Zero Turn: How to Build a Successful Lawn Care Business

MIKE ANDES

CONTENTS

1   Done With the 9 to 5 Job   1

2   Getting the Business Started   19

3   Hiring the First Employee   30

4   The Collision   50

5   The Business on Life-Support   63

6   Creating Systems-Centric Business   76

7   Building a Brand   87

8   Back at Square One   100

9   A New Business, A New Mindset   108

10   Going Beyond Lawn Care Services   118

    The Finish Line   125

CHAPTER 1: DONE WITH THE 9 TO 5 JOB

It was a crisp, spring evening. Leaves were budding from the trees, and the grass was green again. Getting home from a long day of work, Larry pulled his boots off at the entryway, causing dirt to sprinkle along the tile. He smelled chicken and potatoes wafting through the apartment while he was brushing off grass from his work pants. His wife Savannah asked how his day was, dishing him a plate as he sat down at the dinner table.

"It was good, we finished a lot of small jobs today," he said. "What's up with you? How was your day?"

Savannah sat down with him, bringing them both glasses of water. She tried to come up with something to say to him that would provide a good transition for the news she was dying to share. It was important. She needed to do this right.

"Well work was pretty normal. Nothing too crazy," she said, smiling.

"What's on your mind?" Larry asked between bites of mashed potatoes.

Maybe this was the transition she was looking for.

"Actually," she said. "I have some big news."

Larry stopped eating. He was so curious. Savannah's grin had gotten bigger and he had no idea why. Savannah took a deep breath and grabbed Larry's hands, making his thoughts run wild with anticipation.

Whatever it was he could tell it was good… and then it happened.

"I'm pregnant," she said, squeezing his hands lightly.

Larry's heart dropped to his stomach. That was not the news he was expecting. *"It's not bad news,"* he thought, but it did make him nervous. *"Say something,"* he told himself.

"I know its a lot to take in," Savannah said. "Don't think about all the financial stuff right now. Just think about the fact that you're gonna be a dad. We will figure everything else out."

Obviously, this was unplanned. Larry and Savannah had just gotten married, and were barely passed their first anniversary — kids weren't even on their radar yet. *"How can I support a family making $20 an hour?"* he thought to himself. *"Savannah will probably need to quit her job. What if she doesn't go back to work for a couple of years?"*

Before this moment, Larry felt like he was doing pretty good for himself. He was promoted to manager at the small lawn care company he'd been working at for a couple of years. He was good at supervising the work. The edges were always trimmed perfectly, the lines sharp and the grass cut even. When he and his crew were finished, they could make anyone's lawn look as curated as a golf course. Larry's experience in the field showed through in his work, and his boss Joe definitely noticed. Overall, things were going well for him.

But now, Larry had to change his calculations. The responsibility of a child entirely changed what it meant to be "doing pretty good." Before, making $20 an hour full-time was satisfactory, and even allowed for some extra spending money — especially since he was mowing 10 lawns in his neighborhood consistently on weekends to make some extra cash.

"Larry?" Savannah said, looking at him expectantly. It had only been a couple seconds, but it felt like hours.

"I can't believe it," Larry said. "I promise, I am super excited, but it really is hard to avoid thinking about..." he paused. "Everything."

Savannah looked at him with deep understanding. She sighed, and he knew she felt the same weird mix of fear and excitement.

"We will be okay, we will figure everything out," Larry said. "I'll figure things out. Don't worry."

In that moment, Larry realized he needed a raise. The problem was, it had been a few years since he started working with Joe, and had already gotten multiple raises to get him to his $20 per hour mark. Larry would have to pull Joe aside the next day at work and make a pretty strong case for himself, he figured. So that's what he did.

The next morning, when he arrived at Joe's house to pick up equipment and rally his crew, he felt pretty confident he could talk Joe into giving him a raise. After all, Larry was a phenomenal employee who had moved up to a managerial role quickly. He was confident Joe would have his back.

The company was small, but never short on work. They had consistent clients, and usually picked up a few in the springtime, which made Joe extra busy. When Larry showed up at Joe's house, he was on the phone with a client. Instead of prepping the trailer for the days work, Larry walked straight up to Joe, who noticed the approach and stopped what he was doing.

"Hey Larry, what do you need?" Joe asked.

"Actually, I just need a second to talk to you before heading out," Larry said. "The job we're working on is going to take most the day, so I don't know if I'd be able to catch you later, and it's really important."

"Okay, but we gotta make it quick," Joe said, shoving his cell phone into his back pocket.

Larry took a deep breath.

"Joe, I need a raise," he said. "I know I am worth more, and I know I need more. I just found out yesterday Savannah and I have a baby on the way."

Joe raised his eyebrows, then smiled.

"Wow Larry, that's great for you guys!" he said, reaching out to give him a congratulatory hug. Then, he pulled back, with his hands on Larry's shoulders. "But Larry, you know I can't bump your wage. There's no way. I just can't afford it." Joe gave Larry a pat on his left shoulder, then dropped his hands back to his sides. His cell phone starting ringing, and Joe pulled it back out of his pocket.

"Sorry Larry, I have to take this," he said. "Good luck out there today!" Joe turned around and jogged off as he picked up another call from a client.

Larry was dumbfounded. Feelings of anger, frustration and resentment started to well up in his chest. He turned around and walked towards the trailer, which his crew members Pedro and Ben had hooked up to the truck. They were already loading it with equipment, and getting close to finishing, too. Larry slowly made his way toward them, trying to bring his mind back to the day ahead of him, which seemed to pass in a whirlwind.

He mowed lawns with his headphones in, turning up the music so it blasted louder than the sound of the mower. Larry let his muscle memory take over, totally disconnecting from the work — by the end of the day, his body was tired but his brain was totally alert. Larry, Pedro and Ben dropped everything back off at Joe's house, and headed home.

Walking up the stairs to the door of his apartment, Larry sighed, realizing he needed a new plan. He wasn't sure what to do next. Savannah was at the door when he opened it, and she kissed him. Larry decided not to tell her about what happened with Joe … at least not until he had a plan B.

Over the following weekend, Joe left for vacation, and on Monday Larry was responsible for pretty much everything. He took over communicating with clients, organizing job routes and making estimates, and he had to do it all for the whole week. So on top of managing his coworkers and being responsible for ensuring they did everything right, he was acting like the boss. This was the first time Joe had gone on vacation, and left Larry in charge of the business, and the timing couldn't have been worse. Larry wasn't looking at Joe with respect anymore, and instead saw all the flaws of Joe and the business.

For instance, while working with Ben that week (who was a newer employee), Larry noticed how much quicker he finished edging, laying down mulch and mowing. He saw Ben slack off a couple of times, and thought, *"If I were Joe, I never would have hired this guy. If I were the boss, I would have found someone with more experience."* In the middle of the week, while Joe was surely lying on a beach somewhere, Larry saw an estimate Joe had written up for one of their clients. It was a for a $3,000 mulch installation. Larry did some rough calculations in his head, coming to the conclusion that Joe would probably pocket $2,000 from that job.

While driving en-route to a clients house for a spring cleanup, one he would be doing alone, he passed by one of their competitors trucks. It was shiny and new, with a large logo in bright yellow and green: Parscapes. Below the company name, it said, "Your Personal Greenskeeper." Next to "Parscapes" was a graphic of a golf ball with a yellow flag, sitting on three curved lines. The workers on site were all wearing matching uniforms, and Larry thought about how different it would be to work for that company. *"The owner must really know what he's doing,"* Larry thought.

On Friday, the last day of filling in for Joe, Larry worked with Ben again. Ben kept checking his phone, pausing each time, and Larry noticed the time started to add up. Larry huffed with frustration and realized he would have to pick up Ben's slack, but he didn't say anything to him, Larry just kept working. When Larry went home at the end of the day, he vented to Savannah.

"I was basically two people this week," he said. "I was me, the manager, but I was also Joe, the boss. I practically ran the business, and it wasn't that hard, but some of my coworkers are real slackers. I don't get why Joe hired Ben." Savannah looked at him disapprovingly.

"You never used to talk about Ben like this, I thought you liked him," she said.

"I do, but his work ethic is pathetic." Larry said. "We did such a simple job today, and he couldn't keep up with his half of the work." The more Larry talked about it, the more frustrated he got.

Over the following weekend, Joe got back from his vacation. Larry was mowing one of his personal client's lawns, and thinking about how great it would be if he had the time to take Savannah on vacation. He imagined laying on a beach somewhere with her, with the sounds of waves crashing ashore, and them not having a care in the world. When he saw Joe's tan on Monday, his jealousy flared up again, on top of the bitterness he felt from being denied a raise last week — resentment he had bottled up. He didn't talk to Joe much that week. He kept his head down and worked, and did everything he could to avoid seeing him.

The vacation daydream turned into a fantasy he relived that night. He dreamed about being able to make plans on a whim, answering to nobody. Savannah didn't have to work, and Larry was a millionaire. They did whatever they wanted, when they wanted, how they wanted — and Larry could easily provide for a kid. Then he saw his baby, and he woke up abruptly.

Sitting straight up, wide awake in the middle of the night, Larry looked around the room. The tiny "master" bedroom in their tiny apartment, that he hadn't noticed was so small until Savannah told him she was pregnant, seemed to close in on him. However, the unit was unique. They were lucky enough to find a place with a garage — each unit was on the second story, with garages below. All of a sudden, an idea knocked the wind out of him.

What if I start my own business.

Larry layed back down, and let the glorious thought of being his own boss wash over him. He looked over at Savannah before he fell back asleep, absorbed in a new dream he had never had before. No more Joe. No more Ben. No more scraping by with only a little bit of money left over each month to spend.

The next morning, Savannah left for work early, and Larry started the day later. Thoughts were popping up in his brain that seemed to be coming from nowhere, all motivated by the entrepreneurial dream he had the night before. Feeling like a new man, Larry decided he would go to the bank and apply for a personal loan. *"Businesses don't start without capital,"* Larry thought.

When he got to the bank, he parked his car outside of the large gray building, and walked in the door with his head held high. He was dressed in his dirty work pants, surrounded by clean-cut people who probably worked in cubicles, and a couple of retired seniors. Even though Larry stuck out like a sore-thumb, he was confident. He got to the front of the line, and a woman with a plaque that read "WENDY" called him to her desk.

"How can I help you today sir?" Wendy said.

"I need a personal loan," Larry said. "I think I want to try my hand at starting a lawn care business." That was the first time he said it out loud, and he liked the sound of it.

"Well how much money are you thinking you'll need?" Wendy said.

"I am looking to start with five grand," Larry said. "I've been a landscaper for a couple of years working for this other guy, and I realized, it's not worth it to work for someone else. I hate being told what to do all the time."

Wendy laughed. "Doesn't sound like too bad of an idea. Let's see what we can do for you." She turned her attention to her computer screen. She asked for two years of his income history, two years of his home address history and his social security number. The loan, if Larry got it, would be unsecured, meaning he would not provide collateral the bank could take if he didn't pay it back. It would also have a 15% interest rate, and needed to be paid back within three years, so it was on a 36-month schedule. *"Three years from now, I will have a successful business,"* Larry thought, confident he would be able to repay the debt. He thanked Wendy, signed the application and headed straight to work, crossing his fingers hoping he would be approved for the loan.

Arriving at Joe's house, Larry was a bit late. Pedro and Ben were already done connecting the trailer and loading up equipment for the mulch installation job they were supposed to do today.

"Come on Larry, we're burning daylight," Pedro yelled.

"Yeah, I'm coming," Larry hollered back, picking up his pace.

Once they checked to make sure they had everything they needed, the crew hopped into the truck, with Larry in the driver's seat. It stunk like dirt and sweat, as always. The old cloth seats just seemed to absorb the smell of the work. As Larry turned the key in the ignition, the engine whined, but didn't start. He held the key there until the engine finally ignited, growling to life. He was reminded of the trucks owned by Parscapes, and thought, *"When I start my business, I won't buy old useless trucks."*

"Dude, these old trucks are such junk, Joe needs to get nicer stuff," Pedro said, huffing in the back.

On the drive from Joe's garage to the client's house, which was in the center of a big gated neighborhood, Larry thought back to his conversation with Joe, and how quickly his ask for a raise was shut down weeks ago. They passed by the the local outdoor equipment shop, Carl's Mower, on the way to the job, which had shiny, brand-new equipment lined up out front — Larry remembered how old and dirty Joe's equipment was. Pedro was right, Joe needed to buy new stuff. *"My equipment will be so much better,"* he thought.

The crew pulled up to the gate and entered the code, watching the big elegant metal doors open slowly for them to pull into the expensive, highly manicured neighborhood. Driving passed pristine properties, Larry thought about how much these clients paid to have their lawns kept so perfectly trimmed and landscaped. He thought about how much this next job probably cost the client, and how much of that money he, Pedro and Ben weren't going to see.

"Joe is making so much money," Larry thought. As the crew pulled up to the clients beautiful three story house on at least three acres, he felt even more frustrated. Larry, Ben and Pedro were going to be at this property for between five and six hours installing 20 yards of bark mulch around all the flower beds there, and trimming a small hedge of boxwood plants, while Joe was at home raking in the dough.

They parked along the road next to the client's property and starting hauling the equipment up the driveway. The crew got to work cleaning up weeds and filling up wheelbarrows of mulch that Larry pushed back and forth. The garden was starting to look beautiful and although he was doing the hard part of the labor, Larry took pride in the change they were making. Larry started to get into the flow of the work, challenging himself to work faster and harder, plugging headphones into his ears and allowing music to fill his mind. Then, Larry's workflow was interrupted by his pride turning back into frustration. He remembered telling Joe, *"I'm worth more,"* and Joe totally blowing him off. He looked at the crew he was supervising and how the work was panning out — *"I am worth more,"* Larry thought.

Pedro noticed Larry wasn't as laser-focused as he usually was. Pedro was pushing the empty wheelbarrow toward Larry to pick up another round of old mulch, but decided they should take a couple minutes to eat their lunches. Pedro tapped Larry on the shoulder, which brought Larry back to the present moment and out of his head.

"It's almost noon, let's eat real quick," Pedro said.

"Yeah, that's a good idea. Tell Ben," Larry said, panting heavily as he slowed down to take a break. He started heading toward the truck to grab his ham sandwich.

"Ben!" Pedro said, raising his voice. "Want to eat?"

Ben, a couple feet ahead of Larry and Pedro working on another section of the garden, shook his head.

"I'm going to eat later, I had a huge breakfast," Ben responded.

Larry was sitting sideways in the passenger seat with the door open, bending over with his elbows resting on his knees while he took bites of his sandwich from a plastic bag. Pedro walked around the front of the truck and opened the driver side door to grab his lunch, a turkey wrap he picked up from a local grocery store. He got in the driver's seat and closed the door. Taking a bite of his wrap, and turned toward Larry, whose back was facing him.

"Okay Larry, you seem off today," Pedro said. "What's going on?"

Larry peeked back at Pedro over his shoulder, surprised he had noticed something was different.

"Uh, well, I'm just thinking a lot about money," Larry said. "I haven't had a chance to tell you this yet, but Savannah dropped a bomb on me a couple of weeks ago."

"Oh yeah?" Pedro said, his interest thoroughly piqued. "What did she say?"

Larry took a second to chew his sandwich before responding.

"She's pregnant," he said.

Surprised, Pedro put his wrap down and pat Larry on the back.

"Congratulations!" He said with real excitement in his voice. "You're going to be a dad, that's crazy!"

Larry finished his sandwich and turned in the passenger's seat to face forward, crumpling up the sandwich bag and shoving it in his pocket. He didn't want to tell Pedro that he asked Joe for a raise, or that he was interested in starting his own business. He hadn't even told Savannah.

"Yeah, it is. I am excited, don't get me wrong," Larry said. "I'm just nervous I guess."

"I would be too, I have no idea how it feels to expect a kid, but I wish you luck," Pedro said. He finished his lunch too, ending their conversation.

"Thanks Pedro, I appreciate it," Larry said.

When they got back to work, Larry noticed Ben had started trimming the boxwood plants. Ben had only trimmed hedges a couple of times, so Larry was a little irritated he started without telling him. While Pedro got to work edging the garden, Larry walked over to Ben to make sure he was doing things right.

"Ben, why didn't you tell me you were going to start trimming the hedges?" Larry yelled over the whirring of the trimmer.

Ben turned off the hedge trimmer so he could respond.

"Sorry Larry, I thought you'd be happy I was getting this over with," Ben said.

Larry quickly looked over the work Ben had finished so far. There didn't seem to be any issues, and it looked clean. Larry shrugged and decided there was no harm done, even though Ben wasn't a very experienced trimmer.

"It's okay, you know what, I am happy you're getting the job over with," Larry said. "Thanks."

Ben gave Larry a thumbs up and turned on the hedge trimmer again. Larry left him to it and decided he would focus on installing the mulch with Pedro. There was a lot to apply, and they hadn't even started. Larry got back into a workflow, pushing wheelbarrows full of new mulch to the garden, dumping it out and raking it out with Pedro's help. He had his headphones back in, and he was focused again. Somehow, telling Pedro what he was thinking had seemed to help.

It was getting later in the afternoon, and Ben had not yet completed the trimming of the boxwood hedge, and Larry and Pedro had gotten about half of the mulch installed. It was looking good, but taking too long. Larry texted Joe to let him know things weren't going as quickly as planned.

At about five o'clock , they were completely finished, loaded up and ready to drop everything back off at Joe's house. They were all pretty tired. The other crew members, John and George, had already finished up their jobs for the day and were at home enjoying their evenings. Joe was waiting in the garage when they pulled up, and he didn't look too happy. Pedro elbowed Larry, pointing it out.

"I wonder why Joe looks like such a downer," he said.

Pedro and Ben headed home while Larry put the equipment away. Joe told Larry to stop what he was doing, and called him over — he pulled up a picture on his phone and told Larry to look at it. It showed wooden post with a chip taken out of it at the job site Larry, Ben and Pedro were just at.

"I'm not sure how this happened, but the client just emailed me this picture. You were responsible for watching the guys, so I need you to go back to the job and fix this," Joe said. "Just use wood filler and paint over it. I told the client we would get it done."

Joe went back in his house, leaving Larry to finish cleaning up and head back to the job. Larry didn't get back to the site until about 6 p.m., and he wasn't finished until after 7 p.m. He called Savannah, who had been texting him, to let her know why he was so late. When he dropped off the equipment at Joe's house, he could see Joe and his family eating dinner together through the window, enjoying their evening as a family while Larry was still working. By the time he made it home, it was dark out, and Savannah had already eaten dinner. *"What a great way to end the week,"* Larry thought to himself sarcastically. Over the weekend, he told Savannah he was thinking about quitting.

"Babe, I don't know if that's the best idea," Savannah said.

"But what if I start my own lawn care business?" Larry said.

"Do you know how to do that? You've never run a business before," Savannah said. "I'm not trying to crush your dreams, I just think you should give it some more thought before you make any decisions. We are having a child in the next eight months."

"I know, that's why I need to do this," Larry said. "Do you think I could support us with a kid making $20 an hour? No way. And I already asked Joe for a raise — he won't bump me."

"When did that happen? Why didn't you tell me?" Savannah was shocked.

"I didn't want you to worry. And I still don't want you to worry. I am going to quit, and I am going to start my own business, and we will make the most money we ever have," he promised.

On Monday morning, he showed up at Joe's house, but he wasn't dressed for work. All of the anger and resentment he had felt the past few weeks melted away, and was replaced by pure excitement. Larry was never going to work for anyone ever again. Passing by all his coworkers as they were preparing for the day, he headed straight toward Joe, who was of course on the phone. Tapping Joe on the shoulder, he turned around and looked Larry up and down. He motioned with his hand, telling Larry he would be off the phone in a second. Once Joe hung up, putting his cell phone in his pocket, Larry didn't even give him a chance to speak.

"Joe, I quit. I'm starting my own lawn care business," Larry said defiantly. "You better watch out, because you might just lose yours."

Joe's jaw dropped in shock. Larry just smirked —
he was ready to work for himself,
and thought, *"boy, that felt good!"*

CHAPTER 2: GETTING THE BUSINESS STARTED

The sun streamed in through the bedroom window of Larry and Savannah's apartment. It was spring, but it was getting closer to summer. Birds were chirping while the two of them got ready for the day. Larry made them breakfast — scrambled eggs, bacon and pancakes... on a weekday! He was feeling great about his decision to quit working for Joe, and riding the high. Savannah still wasn't too sure, but she trusted Larry's judgement. When she left for work, Larry began planning his next steps.

"What should I name my business?" Larry thought, sitting in his pajamas on the couch. After juggling a couple of ideas, he landed on something simple: **Larry's Lawn Care.** Springing to his feet, energized by realizing his business now had an identity, he grabbed his laptop and started researching what else he would need to start. After reading a couple of articles, he decided he would register a business license and sole-proprietorship legal entity structure. Larry filled out an online application, paid the $99 fee, and clicked "Submit."

Feeling elated, he logged into his social media accounts and started posting about his new endeavor, to make sure everyone knew he was going to be his own boss. He updated his status so he was labeled an entrepreneur, and the comments and likes started rolling in. Larry smiled and shut his laptop, feeling good about the way his friends and family were receiving the news. He cleaned up the dishes from breakfast, then made himself a cup of coffee and grabbed his keys to go check the mail. *"This Tuesday feels like a Sunday,"* he thought.

Letters started spilling out of the mailbox as soon as he opened the door. They hadn't checked the mail in at least a week… *"too busy working for the the man"* Larry thought. He grabbed the stack of envelopes and brought them back into the apartment, sifting through the junk until he found a letter from the bank. Larry's heart skipped a beat. Ripping it open, he pulled the letter from the envelope and unfolded it. With the letter lying flat on the table, his eyes immediately were drawn to one word: **approved.** The new loan would put $5,000 in his bank account, and he only had to pay back $175 a month for it. *"How can this day get any better?"* he thought to himself.

That letter stoked the fire of freedom that Larry had kindled. Larry had the capital he needed to start building his business, and he imagined growing an empire. He texted Savannah to tell her the good news, which he hoped would help reassure her that he knew what he was doing. Now that he had money, he could go buy equipment. Larry got dressed and head out to Carl's Mower, which had everything from push mowers, to zero-turns and trailers. With the approval letter in his pocket, Larry pulled up to the business. *"Joe will be so jealous,"* Larry thought.

The shop was full of state-of-the-art equipment. Larry started creating a list in his mind, trying to think of all the stuff he would need, but he couldn't keep track of everything. *"I really gotta write this all down,"* Larry thought to himself. He walked up to the front desk and asked for a pen, and the desk attendant gave him one.

"Do you have a piece of paper I can use?" Larry asked the attendant, who shook his head no. Larry shrugged and pulled the approval letter from his pocket, using the back of it to list what he needed. Starting with the expensive stuff, he listed everything. He needed a zero turn mower, a truck and a trailer for sure. Then he needed a push mower, a weedeater, blower and edger. Searching the shop, he realized all of it would add up quickly. Larry left a space next to each line item so he could fill in the costs as he went.

At Carl's Mower, he knew he could get the zero-turn, trailer and everything else on the list, besides the truck. He asked the attendant about how financing works.

"You don't have to give us a penny today," the attendant said. "We do 0% down financing."

That was music to Larry's ears. Starting outside, he looked at the big stuff that would need to be financed: the zero-turns and the trailer. He decided on a top of the line 60-inch zero-turn mower, with a $12,000 price tag. His monthly payment would be about $330 for three years, which he considered doable. Looking at the trailers, there were open and closed options, and he sat down to think about the pros and cons for a bit.

Open-air trailers are lighter in weight and cheaper. They also allow wind to cool down the engines of the equipment while driving down the road. Open-air landscape trailers make it easier and faster to get weed wackers and blowers from the racks. However, it's open to the elements — rocks, rain, snow, etc. — and it would be best to store it in his garage, if it fits. Enclosed trailers are heavy and more expensive, but they protect equipment from weather and don't have to be stored indoors.

After weighing the pros and cons for a couple of minutes, Larry decided to go for the open-air, 7 by 14 foot trailer. He wanted to be able to afford to get a decent truck later, so it made more sense to cut costs on the trailer. He picked one with a $5,000 price tag. With the financing plan, it would cost him about $140 a month for three years. He figured the neighbors wouldn't mind if the trailer was in his driveway, and he could just put a tarp over it… saving him from the need to buy an enclosed trailer.

Moving down the list, Larry decided to pay cash for some of the other items he needed, since he had $5000 at his disposal. He looked around the shop and found a $1,200 push mower, $500 weed eater, $600 blower and a $400 edger that met his standards. By this point, he had $2,300 left, so he started grabbing hand tools — shovels, rakes, wheelbarrows, a chainsaw, etc. — which amounted to around $600.

He headed over to the clothing section of the store and decided to splurge on some nice boots, since his were totally tattered. The best pair were full grain leather work boots that felt as though they were molded to Larry's feet. They were $230, but he thought, *"I deserve these. Besides, I'll use them everyday, they're an investment."* He added a sweater, new hat, pair of pants and glasses to his shopping cart. Then Larry picked up small items he thought of, like shears, gas cans and oil. Overall, his cash total at Carl's Mower was $4,300. The last piece of equipment Larry needed was a truck, so he decided to look at a local dealership during the week. He was close to having all the equipment he needed.

Some of his stuff he could fit in his car, but the bigger equipment had to be delivered. Luckily, Carl's Mower offered that too. He stuffed everything he could into his trunk and back seat, and drove home, with the delivery guy on his tail. They set up the trailer in the driveway, putting most of the equipment on the racks, and put the rest of the small stuff in their one-car garage.

When he walked into the apartment, it was mid-afternoon, and Savannah was on her way home. Larry had accomplished a lot and was excited to tell her all about it. He started making dinner when she walked in.

"I see you went on a shopping spree," she said, referring to the new equipment in the driveway. "How much did all that stuff cost?"

"It didn't cost us anything, really," Larry said. "I will be paying it off monthly with the income from the business. I can cover it all with just the ten weekend clients I already have." Savannah looked relieved after hearing that.

They enjoyed a nice dinner, talked about their days and started guessing whether or not their child would be a boy or a girl. It was one of the best days of Larry's life.

All throughout that week, Larry worked on getting the business going. He visited a local car dealership next to find a truck he could drive to jobs — all of his clients were within a walks distance from his apartment, and he had been previously mowing them with his own residential mower.

When he got to the dealership, Larry was overwhelmed with options. Walking around the lot, the first vehicle that caught his eye was a brand new $50,000 dump truck. It was tempting to take a closer look. However, $50,000 was way too expensive, and Larry knew that, so he kept walking toward the end of the lot where the used trucks were lined up to see what was available at a lower price range. There was a 15 year old truck… it was priced at $5,000.

The truck had a lot of miles on it, and Larry could see it was not just used, but well used. However, it looked functional. It would serve the purpose of a lawncare business, but was similar to the trucks Larry had driven when he worked for Joe, which he and his coworkers always complained about. Remembering the finicky starters and the stench of the cabin from dirty laborers, Larry couldn't entertain the thought of buying a low-end truck like that, so he kept looking.

In the middle of the lot, he saw a nice looking truck with the price emblazoned on the windshield in yellow for $20,000. *"That's not too bad,"* Larry thought to himself. He walked up to the truck and examined it. The paint was perfect, the seats were black leather, and the body pristine. It was only a couple years old. *"This truck was probably one of the best on the market the year it came out,"* Larry thought to himself, justifying the higher price. By the time the salesman walked up to him, Larry had already made up his mind.

"Good morning, sir," The salesman said. "Taking a liking to the truck?"

"It looks real good," Larry said. He paused, looking back at the truck, and decided to move forward. "I'm interested in financing this bad boy."

The salesman smiled, and told Larry to come into the office so they could run the numbers. They sat down at a desk and discussed the options, and Larry told him he wanted to finance the whole thing. When everything was said and done, Larry had another debt to pay. He financed the $20,000 truck for five years at 5.5% interest, with a monthly payment of about $380 per month. That's fine, he decided, *"I'll make that with just a couple more clients each month."* Larry drove the truck off the lot and headed home, excited about his new venture and ready to take on the world.

Larry parked the new truck in his driveway and got it hooked up to the trailer he had purchased from Carl's. The next step was to start marketing. *"I've only got my ten weekend clients,"* he thought. *"I need to get the word out. How does Joe market to people?"* Larry racked his brain to see if he could recall marketing strategies Joe used. He was coming up short, because he had never really asked Joe how they gained new clients, and he had never helped with advertising the company. After doing a bit of research, he decided he would post flyers around town.

Larry had $500 left from his personal loan. He used that money to design and order a couple thousand flyers, along with some business cards. The flyers would say "LARRY'S LAWN CARE" in large bold letters at the top, and offer new customers a free lawn service. It included a list of services he was prepared to offer, his cell phone number, and a stock image of someone's lawn to provide visual appeal.

Throughout the week, he drove around nearby neighborhoods and posted the new flyers wherever he could. He put them on street lights and fences, and found coffee shops with community boards that he pinned them to. He handed out business cards everywhere he went, telling people from grocery store clerks to his personal barber about his new business. He started to get a couple calls from prospective clients here and there, and thought the advertising was really working well.

When the weekend rolled around again, he showed up to his clients homes with his brand new truck, trailer and equipment. Larry looked and felt super professional. He had been mowing these neighbors lawns for a couple of years consistently, and they all loved his work, so they were excited to hear Larry was starting his own business. Some of them congratulated him, even asking to take a picture with Larry in front of his new truck and trailer, holding up one of the flyers.

Larry made sure all his customers knew he was available for more work, and asked them if other neighbors would be interested. One of his long-time clients, Lacey, texted her next-door neighbor about it while Larry was mowing her lawn. The neighbor showed up half-way through the job, asking Larry if he would mow his lawn weekly, and how much he would charge for it. Larry stopped mowing and took a peak next door, seeing that the lawn was very similar to Lacey's. *"I charge Lacey $20, so I guess I can charge this guy the same price,"* Larry thought to himself, worried he would lose the customer if he didn't give him a quick answer.

"I'll do it for $20," Larry said. The guy seemed impressed with the price, and they shook on it.

"Twenty bucks it is!" he said. "I'll see you next week then? I would prefer you come on the weekdays while I am at work."

"Awesome, I will be there Monday!" Larry's smile was huge, and his confidence boosted. He went back over to Lacey's house to finish up her lawn, and started adding the job to his calendar. He put the guy's address in, but then realized he hadn't caught his name or his phone number. He labeled the entry "Lacey's neighbor lawn mow."

Throughout the first week of his business getting up and running, Larry's Lawn Care gained seven clients. He typically quoted them $20 to $30 for each mowing service, using what he charged his current clients to help base his prices off of. He was on a roll. Larry kept up with the flyers, and his cell phone started to ring constantly.

He mostly offered mowing, weeding and trimming services, as well as clean-ups. As the summer heat picked up, so did the work. Though the money was rolling in, the bank account never seemed to grow, but that didn't concern him. He was busy all the time, building relationships with clients and always impressing them with his superior work — especially with his relatively low charge.

But after a few months, Savannah started to notice the savings was stagnant, even though Larry's business was bringing in around $4,000 per month in gross revenue. She didn't like how often he was gone, either. One evening, Larry got home really late. He wasn't able to eat dinner with her that night, so she had ordered pizza and saved some for him. When he got home, he reheated some of it, and Savannah decided to open a conversation about his absence.

"I don't like how often you're gone," she said. "And it seems like we haven't been able to save money anymore."

Larry assured her this was only a short-term issue, and that the business was still really young.

"We just have to be patient. We'll be able to save way more than ever before soon," he said.

Savannah seemed half-way convinced, crossing her arms and leaning back in her chair. Larry could tell she was mulling it over.

"When you have more clients, you're just going to be busier though. If this is what 17 clients is like, how much will you be working with more?"

Larry put his hand on her shoulder.

"No matter how busy I get, I'll always have time for you," he said. "And the baby."

She smiled and looked down at her growing stomach, reminded of the child they would be having at the end of the year. It seemed like she was convinced. During that conversation, Larry could not have anticipated how much business would be booming by the end of the summer. He continued to place flyers around town every week, and got referrals from customers due to the impressive quality of his work, and his affordable prices. By September, Larry was working 80-hour weeks and had accumulated 30 clients. He stopped accepting new clients too, since he was pretty maxed out. Larry's Lawn Care was off to an impressive start.

CHAPTER 3: HIRING THE FIRST EMPLOYEE

Leaves had changed colors, from green to red hues, oranges and yellows. The sunlight changed qualities, coming from a different angle in the sky, and the air started to cool. It was fall, and Larry was driving to one of his clients properties to start the day. On the way there, he happened to drive past his old coworkers — they were laboring away on a fall clean up job, looking tired and unhappy. He saw the old, run-down truck parked by the property, and he couldn't help but smirk. *"I am so happy that's not me,"* he thought.

It was early November, and he was on track to make $6,000 that month. If he were still working for Joe, he would be bringing in a quarter of that. His chest was puffed with pride, realizing how far he had come in just a couple of months. His customers are loyal, and they love him, and his work. He hadn't had a single complaint, and with every job he was a perfectionist. He treated the work like an art, and clients noticed.

While he raked piles of leaves up and threw them into trash bags, he started thinking about where Larry's Lawn Care was headed. He was thinking about the massive growth, and high income potential. At the rate things were going now, he was poised for taking over the market, he thought. It was a really good day, and not just because of his business' bright future.

At this point, Savannah was in her third-trimester of pregnancy. She was becoming fatigued more easily, and working seemed to strain her, though she never complained. Larry intentionally planned a short work day because there was an important doctor's appointment they were going to in the afternoon. They would find out if their baby was a boy or a girl.

He cleaned up the equipment and putting everything away by 3 p.m., threw his work clothes in the wash, and changed into a button up and jeans. Savannah met him at home, glowing with excitement, and they drove to the clinic together. After sitting for what felt like hours in the waiting room, a nurse called Savannah's name, and they headed in to get an ultrasound. After the nurse finished chattering away about how healthy the baby looked, the nurse turned to them both with a smile.

"Are you ready to find out the sex?" she asked.

Savannah and Larry unanimously answered: "Yes."

"It's a boy."

The tension in the room broke and Savannah started crying with joy, and Larry hugged her. This was secretly what he'd been hoping to hear. When they got home, they were both riding an emotional wave, and couldn't stop smiling. They went out to dinner to celebrate, and that's when Larry decided he would ask Savannah if she wanted to quit her job.

"The business is booming," Larry told her. "You can quit!"

Savannah grabbed his hands across from the dinner table at the restaurant.

"That. Sounds. Amazing," she said, imagining the load of work off her shoulders.

"Wouldn't it be?" Larry said. "You can spend more time with our boy."

Savannah agreed she would put in her two weeks the next day. It was one of the best days of their lives. They talked about the future that night, and about Larry's grandiose dreams for his lawn care business. At this point, Savannah was trusting in the business' trajectory, and they had bet their livelihood on its long-term success. **Little did Larry know that things were about to change.**

* * *

The first frost came near the end of the month, but there was still plenty of lawn care work to do. Larry's phone was pretty quiet, he wasn't getting as many calls as usual. He started to wonder why things were slowing so much.

One day in the beginning of December, he had no work planned. It wasn't intentional — there was literally nothing for him to do. He was kind of happy about it however, because he hadn't really had a day off since he started the business. It gave him a chance to wash his equipment, which he loved doing. For hours, he washed the truck, the mowers and the zero-turn. Then he took extra time to dutifully wipe them down with microfiber cloths, reaching every corner, nook and cranny. Since he had the day to himself, he even waxed and buffed them until they shined as if they were brand new. Savannah came outside to see how he was doing, and noticed how nice the equipment was looking.

"It all looks just like when you first brought it home," she said, blown away.

The next day came around, and he still Larry had no work to complete. But this time, he couldn't spend the day cleaning the equipment. Larry started to get nervous, realizing this might be a trend. He called his clients for more work, asking if they needed their gutters cleaned or leaves raked, or if they needed any bush trimming done. He didn't get many takers, but some said yes and scheduled work for the remainder of the week.

Putting the numbers together, Larry got a little bit stressed. December is expensive for most people due to the holiday season. He hadn't had time to pick up Christmas gifts yet, and was planning on spending a lot this year on Savannah and the baby. There was only a few weeks until Christmas too. Plus, the baby would be coming soon. By the middle of the month, he knew he wasn't going to make more than $3,000 total. Savannah noticed that their bank account wasn't looking too good.

"Hey Larry?" Savannah said, sitting down next to him on the couch one night. "I saw that when the bills pulled, our account dropped. It hasn't dropped like this since you started the business, really."

CHRISTMAS EVE

Savannah was making Christmas cookies, and the sweet smell enveloped the apartment. She pulled them out of the oven to cool, when she started to feel a dull ache in her lower back and abdomen. Then she doubled over in pain, leaning against the kitchen counter for support. Larry immediately knew she was going into labor, and his heart started thumping hard in his chest — the baby was a few weeks early.

They took the car and rushed to the emergency room, Larry speeding the whole drive. When they got there, Savannah was immediately put into a wheelchair and brought to a delivery room. Larry called family members and friends to let them all know the baby was coming, and posted on social media so everyone knew he was about to be a dad. He was ecstatic. However, some of his original fears returned.

Larry had no work scheduled for next week. He had no idea how they were going to afford the medical bills and pay his monthly debts. *"This isn't the time to think about that,"* he thought to himself, frustrated that finances were stressing him out at one of the most important moments of his life. It was just like when she first told him she was pregnant, but this time he had a lot more responsibilities and he was self-employed.

After hours and hours of stressful anticipation, they had a beautiful baby boy early Christmas morning.

They heard him cry for the first time. Savannah, exhausted yet renewed, held their son against her chest. Larry couldn't believe his eyes.

"What should we name him?" Larry asked Savannah.

She contemplated for a minute, looking at his little face and trying to see what matched.

"I think he's a James," Savannah said.

"I think so too," Larry said, kissing his son's forehead.

That Christmas was unforgettable. But the following week, though Larry was happy he was able to spend time with his newborn baby boy, the financial anxiety built every day that he wasn't out working. The bills were stacking up, and with all his payments and medical bills, Larry was struggling. He just couldn't pay it. After the new year passed, Larry headed to the bank to see if he could talk to Wendy, and tell her his situation.

Walking into the bank, he looked around to see if Wendy was working. She was at the end of the counter, so Larry hopped in line. Approaching the front, Wendy called him over to her desk, recognizing who he was.

"Larry, it's good to see you again," she said.

"How's the business venture going?"

With his elbows on the counter Larry pressed his face into his hands, then looked back up at Wendy, trying to compose himself. "It was doing great a few months ago, but the winter has been really rough," he said. "On top of that, my wife had a baby Christmas morning."

Wendy clapped her hands together with a smile of disbelief, breaking from her calm customer service demeanor for a moment. "Oh my gosh! That is so awesome, your Christmas gift was a baby!" Wendy tried to calm her giddiness, clearing her throat. "Well, a million congratulations to you and your wife. But what can I do for you today?"

Larry laughed nervously, happy she seemed to care about them. *"Maybe she will help me,"* he thought. "Well, the bills are getting overwhelming. I haven't had any work for about a week, but I really needed it, and I was expecting the baby to come in January," he said. "I wasn't super prepared to start paying big hospital bills. Is there any way you can cut me a break on the personal loan payments? If I could take that off my plate for a couple of months, it would help a lot." Wendy was empathetic, but reserved. She wanted to help, Larry could tell.

"Larry, the only thing I can do is cut down your payments so you only cover the cost of interest," Wendy said. "That would save you a little over $100 a month, but you still have to pay the leftover $60 bucks or so."

Larry sighed in relief. "Anything would help at this point," he said.

"If we cut down the payments through April, will you be able to pay the full amount again in the spring?" Wendy asked.

"Yes, absolutely yes," Larry assured her. "Spring is super busy for lawn care, and I have like 30 clients who will need work done… there's just not much they need done right now."

"Wow, that's a lot of properties for one guy," Wendy said. "You must be busy. Are you going to be able to spend time with your wife and kid once business picks up again?"

Larry paused. He had been so concerned about needing work that he hadn't really thought through the fact that he was probably going to be be back working 80-hour weeks in the spring.

"I'm sure I will make it work," he said, scratching the back of his head. He wasn't actually sure.

"You know what you should do?" Wendy said, leaning in closer over the counter. "You should hire an employee. That way you won't have to be out in the field all the time."

Larry was floored. *"How had I not thought of that?"* he asked himself. Leaving the bank he knew that hiring an employee was what he was going to have to do. He could expand the clientele and start bringing in more money, and easily pay for an employee. He knew just who to hire, too.

When April came around and business started to pick back up, he called his friend Brad from highschool and asked if he would help him out for $12.50 an hour, under the table. He was a good friend, and said yes. That allowed Larry to start soliciting new clients, because he just doubled his production.

They worked well together, doing jobs quickly and efficiently. Eventually, Larry was able to put more of his focus on the clients, invoicing and paperwork. While Brad did the brunt of the lawn work, Larry would take phone calls and respond to emails on site, while intermittently helping Brad with the lawn care. They drove around in the truck together for every job, and as Spring moved toward summer, Larry had accumulated 50 clients and was pulling in $10,000 a month in revenues.

In July, he started to get burnt out though. Balancing the physical demands of the lawncare with the constant client communication began to weigh on him. The stress came to a head when Savannah pointed out how distant he was — this time, she was genuinely angry with him.

"You're never home at a decent time, you hardly spend any time with James and you're always distracted," she fumed. "I don't think you've made it to a single doctor check-up for him either since you hired Brad."

Larry knew she was right, and immediately shifted to damage control. "I am so sorry Savannah, I will make sure to be there for you and James," he said.

"You're apology is not enough," she said. "You need to come up with a plan to get the work off your back. You also need to look at the business finances, because I haven't seen any growth in profit since you increased your workload."

Larry thought about it for a moment. *"Okay, I gotta hire a second person,"* he thought to himself. With a second employee he could pull out of the field and really focus on the clients and marketing, and could improve overall profits, he thought.

"I know what I'm going to do," Larry said. "I will hire a second person, increase clientele and get out of the field as much as I can. Then, I'll take us all on a vacation in September."

"Hook, line and sinker," he thought, proud of his new plan, and happy to see Savannah back on board.

Looking for a second employee turned out to be a lot more difficult than he had imagined during their conversation. He didn't have another friend like Brad interested in working with him under the table, which meant he had to start looking to hire strangers. He posted ads online that got a number of responses, but most didn't seem like real leads. Larry sifted through the lot and found five people that seemed promising, setting up interviews with all of them at McDonald's.

To his dismay, only one guy showed up. He seemed untrustworthy and didn't have any work history, and Larry wasn't sure he could withstand hours of physical labor anyway. Larry lost some of his optimism, and started to become discouraged, but he went through more emails that night and saw five more people respond to his ad that actually seemed like good candidates. He set up more interviews at McDonald's for the next day.

This time, two out of five showed up. *"Why do people agree to meet somewhere if they aren't actually going to show up?"* Larry thought, annoyed. The first guy was just as unsuitable as the last — no work history, no references and, frankly, unlikeable. But the second guy he interviewed had a great personality. His name was Marvin.

Marvin had work history. He bounced around the construction industry, working for several places, each a few months at a time. He didn't provide references, but Larry assumed he would be a good worker. The guy looked strong and capable. He knew the lack of references and the dodgy work history were red flags, but trusted the guy anyway. Larry also had no desire to continue searching for an employee, with how poorly the interview process had already gone.

Larry hired Marvin on the spot, and by the end of July, Larry and bother of his workers were mowing, raking and digging together. They piled into the truck to each job, and Larry no longer had to help with the labor. He dropped off the guys at each job, let them do the work while he put almost all his focus on his growing customer base. Now, Larry's Lawn Care had 70 clients — seven times what Larry started with last year when he first started the business.

But things weren't exactly perfect. With Brad and Marvin working together, typically unsupervised by Larry, Brad started to complain about Marvins work ethic.

"He's not horrible, but he's not the best," Brad said. "I see him on his phone a lot, and he's kinda lazy. I typically pick up his slack. Oh, and he smokes on the job."

Larry told Brad to keep him in the loop about it, but didn't bring it up with Marvin. He didn't want to make Marvin mad and lose him, especially now that there was tons of work to be done. He also feared what would happen if he had to spend the time looking for a new employee, on top of doing all the mowing jobs and communicating with clients. So he basically let the complaints go, and Brad didn't bring it up again. At least, not yet.

With the three guys all working, Larry's Lawn Care was at $14,000 in revenue per month, and Larry was bringing home a good profit again. Feeling positive about his business, he started thinking about next steps for growth. How could he improve efficiency? How could he improve profits even more? And how could he get out of the field and achieve the vacation he promised Savannah?

Transportation was the central issue, he determined. With one truck, they all had to drive together to each job, which reduced efficiency and kept Larry driving around with them. He needed to get a second truck so he could send them out on their own, leaving him with a truck to do estimates, material deliveries, and payment pickup. Larry went back to the dealership he bought his first truck at, and financed another one of equal value, adding an additional $380 monthly payment.

With two trucks, Brad and Marvin could be at different jobs all day, which would really improve their productivity. The morning after bringing the second truck hom, he unveiled it to Marvin and Brad, and explained that Brad would drive the old truck, while he and Marvin drove the second one. Sometimes Brad would drive alone, and Marvin would ride with Larry — other times Larry would drive alone to do estimates, while Marvin would ride with Brad. They planned out their routes for the day, and got going.

Brad had mowing jobs scheduled for the whole day — that way it was plug and play for him, and he would probably not need any help from Larry. Marvin had a mulch install to do, which Larry would be available to help with since they were driving together. By the end of the day, Brad had mowed lawns worth $400 altogether, and Marvin completed about $800 worth of mulch installs. Larry's Lawn Care brought in $1,200 revenue, all in *one day*. Now, all of a sudden, Larry was really bringing home the bacon.

"If I could do this every day," Larry thought to himself, feeling elated, *"I could make like $300,000 a year."* Splitting up crews was super profitable, and they kept doing it. After a couple of weeks in the new workflow, there came a day when Larry was done with work by 7 p.m. He wasn't just done mowing and landscaping, cleaning equipment and putting stuff away,

he was done with estimates, paperwork and emails. Larry literally had a couple hours of free time, which hadn't happened since hiring Brad. Larry kicked back on the couch that evening and got to play a board game with Savannah after she put James to bed.

"Keep this up," Savannah said, feeding him popcorn.

"Don't worry, I'm on a roll," Larry teased. "After this game, let's book that vacation I promised you."

That night, they booked a week-long tropical cruise in late September. While he and Savannah were on vacation, Larry would have to trust his employees to work together without his help, and keep each other on track. By now, it was August, so he had time to prepare. Marvin and Brad worked together, driving the old truck. They had a lot of mowing jobs, but Larry was confident they could finish at a reasonable time, and without needing any help. However, while Larry was running business errands and meeting with clients, he got a text from Brad about Marvin.

"Dude, I don't think we can finish the work. Marvin is smoking on the job and slacking hard," it said. Frustrated, Larry responded, "Tell him to quit smoking and get working." He didn't understand why Brad was complaining to him instead of Marvin. They finished their work on time, so Larry assumed Brad figured out how to deal with it.

As the vacation date approached, Larry felt prepared. He set up the work week for Brad and Marvin to only include mowing jobs — just to be safe. No landscape installs or cleanups. Simple. He checked all the equipment, and made sure all clients were taken care of. This vacation had to make up for all the time he was disengaged from Savannah and James at home, so he needed to be as disconnected from work as possible while they were on the cruise. When they left, Brad assured Larry they wouldn't have any problems. Again, with just mowing, it was plug and play.

The first day on the cruise, they woke up to the soft smell of the sea water breeze wafting into their cabin through the cracked window. Larry prepared to have a fun first day of vacation with his family. The cruise they booked had a nursery on-board too, which meant Savannah and Larry could spend some time alone while eight-month-old James got to play with other kids. *"This is a dream,"* Larry thought.

But when the cruise hit its first stop a couple days later, and passengers offloaded to explore, Larry's phone regained cell service and started to buzz. He had some emails from clients. Luckily they weren't complaints, so he decided to respond when he returned home. At the beach, however, he got an angry voicemail from one his very first clients.

"I'm really disappointed in the service lately," the client said. "Your guys left clippings all over my car after doing a terrible job on the cut in the first place. The lines were uneven and they missed a couple of spots. On top of that, one of them was smoking on my property. I've got kids, I don't want that near my house. "

Larry felt like he was punched in the stomach. This was his first complaint he'd ever received, and he was hundreds of miles away, unable to resolve it himself. The client was a good customer who always loved his work, too. Larry felt horribly out of control. He told Savannah he needed to call Brad, saying it was urgent. Leaving the sand behind, he walked uphill toward the grass and palm trees, so he could call Brad alone. He immediately answered the phone, and Larry went off on him.

"Brad, what's going on?!" he said sternly. "We've never gotten a complaint, and I'm on vacation, I can't deal with this right now."

"Larry I'm sorry but its not my fault. I told you, Marvin's not a good employee," Brad said indignantly. "I try to stay on top of it, but it's hard working with the guy."

"So I assume Marvin was smoking again?" Larry said.

"Yeah man, who else would it be?" Brad said, scoffing.

"Okay well tell him he's gonna have to deal with me if he doesn't quit smoking on clients property," Larry said.

Hanging up, he then proceeded to call the client. Larry apologized profusely, offering him free service and promising there would be no more smoking. He assured the client he would take a look at the lawn when he returned from vacation and fix it.

The next couple of days, trying to enjoy the vacation was torturous for Larry. He couldn't relax, and kept worrying his customers were going to leave him. At night he couldn't sleep, kept awake by concerns about his employees. *"Have they been this bad with all of the clients? What if they get fed up with the service and I lose jobs?"* he thought. He wanted to fire Marvin so bad, but he knew he couldn't, because he needed him to work. In the mornings at the breakfast buffet on the cruise, his worries would return. Sometimes he was positive everything would be fine, and that his customers were overreacting, but other times he thought his employees were single-handedly ruining his business. Savannah could tell a drastic difference between Larry on day one and Larry after the phone call on day three, and tried to help him relieve stress, but nothing seemed to help.

Getting home from the trip, it was early October, and deep into fall. While bringing all their luggage into the apartment and winding down, Larry saw the equipment hooked to the trucks — it was dirty. He examined the mowers, and saw that the blades were dull. *"I leave for one week and they can't keep things clean,"* he thought, shaking his head. Then, he noticed one of the trucks had a long scrape on the drivers side door. And it wasn't the older truck, it was the one he had just bought a few months ago. Turning around with frustration, overwhelmed by the mess he would have to clean up, he decided not to worry about the scrape. He couldn't afford to fix it anyway.

The first day back on the job, Larry caught up on emails and avoided chastising Brad and Marvin until he could get a handle on the business again. Brad worked on his own truck that day, while Larry drove with Marvin. That morning, Brad made a big mistake. Working with a weedeater, a small rock got got in the blades, flinging out and hitting the client's window. The impact shattered it, causing $800 worth of damage that Larry would be liable for. Brad told Larry, who frantically got to work trying to fix it. While trying to juggle monitoring Marvin's work and arranging to have a contractor go fix the window, Larry received *another* client complaint.

The client told Larry that the guys left skid marks on his lawn from the zero-turn mower, and the overall quality of work has declined in the past couple of months. He said Larry's employees don't do a good job, and they are inconsiderate. For example, they keep leaving the backyard gates open, and one of the client's dogs recently got loose. "I just want YOU to do my lawn," the client said urgently. Hearing that was gut wrenching, since Larry felt the same way. Larry started ruminating on all the recent problems, which he never would have had if it was just him mowing and working on the clients' properties. He's never had complaints like this, and he's never broken anything. Again, he avoided confronting Brad and Marvin that evening, because he wasn't ready.

A few weeks later, there came a day when Marvin didn't show up to work, and they had tons of jobs to do. Larry vigorously called and texted him, asking where he was and telling him to get to work as soon as possible. He got no response. Larry had estimates scheduled all day that required him to go to prospective clients homes, so he wasn't able to fill in for Marvin. That meant Brad had double the work to do, but Larry promised he would help as soon as he finished estimates. Larry met up with Brad at a job around 6 p.m. Tired, sweaty and frustrated, Brad finally confronted Larry about how things were going lately.

"Larry, I can't keep working for so cheap," he said. "I know we are friends, but you're ripping me off right now. I'm doing way more than Marvin, and constantly having to keep the guy in check. I redo his work all the time, and today he's not even here!"

Larry could not believe what he was hearing. *"Brad literally broke a client's window yesterday,"* he thought.

"It's not fair that Marvin and I make the same hourly. I need a raise, and I think $20 an hour is perfectly fair," Brad said, crossing his arms.

Larry's jaw dropped, but he tried to contain his astonishment, not wanting to lose Brad. "Uhh… let me think about that," Larry said.

Driving home that night around 8 p.m. after they finally finished all the work, Larry fantasized about firing Brad and Marvin. *"I like Brad, but I can't afford to pay* him $20 an hour," he thought to himself. *"And Marvin doesn't even deserve a job."* Fuming, gripping the wheel with white-knuckles, he kept thinking about how much damage the employees did to his company. *"Plus, someone scratched the new truck…. and Brad just broke a clients window! I can't grow a company with idiots like this. Why don't they work as hard as I do? Why don't they care?"* he thought. But he started considering whether having employees was worth it at all. Larry wasn't bringing home much more in actual profit than he was at the beginning, when he was working alone with fewer clients.

Before employees, Larry was able to do what he loved without the stress of managing people. He was outside every day, and his clients loved his work. He was tired of the phone constantly ringing and doing estimates for new clients. He was tired of entitled employees who didn't care about the work the way Larry did. He began questioning why he thought he needed employees at all. Without employees, he would have less risk, and put more profit in the bank heading into the winter months. *"Besides, work is going to slow down soon, I could barely keep myself busy last winter. There's no way I could keep two employees busy,"* he thought. *"I really just need to fire them anyways."* Pulling into his driveway, Larry made up his mind. Tomorrow, he would be rid of employees.

CHAPTER 4: THE COLLISION

It was cold, and Larry's bedroom window was frosted. He had been working alone since November, and had plenty of jobs over the winter for himself. He wasn't taking any additional customers, so he didn't have as much administrative or customer service stuff to do, and was often home at a good time. James was a year old, and the family was happy.

Larry got out of bed early, and walked to the kitchen to make coffee. Pouring a cup, he could see the steam rising from it as it filed his mug. Peeking out the window, he saw the mail truck leaving the apartment complex, so he went to go check what he'd received. He clutched his coffee mug and braced the January cold.

When he opened the mailbox, there were only a few envelopes. He grabbed them and walked back to his apartment as the sun finally started to rise. In the kitchen he opened a couple — one was a postcard from his mom, others were solicitations from credit card companies. Then he reached a letter from the IRS. He stared at it for a second before tearing it open, and felt a trickle of dread. The letter had some pretty large numbers on it. *"Oooooooh no…."* he thought.

Larry owed $12,000 in sales tax from the previous year.

He slapped the letter down on his kitchen counter, leaning forward with one hand on his forehead. He heard

James waking up and crying, causing Savannah to wake too.

The first year he paid annual sales tax, it was nowhere near this much. So he kind of forgot about it, not realizing how much he was racking up in debt to the IRS every time he made a sale to a customer. This bill was what he owed from his second year in business — that year he had hired and fired two employees, allowing him to grow his customer base and make way more sales.... which meant collecting way more sales tax. The only problem was that that money was already spent. The collected sales tax had been spent on payroll, paying of the loans, and fuel.

This was another setback, but Larry pulled himself together so he could come up with a plan. He still had debt on two trucks, one of them that was no longer necessary since firing his employees, so he planned on putting one up for sale. That would get rid of a $380 monthly bill, then he could pay off the tax debt within the year if he did monthly payments. The budget would be really tight, but he calculated he could handle a monthly $1,000 tax payment.

He decided to sell the old truck since he had paid off more of the debt already. It was in good shape still, and unlike the new truck, it didn't have a scratch. Larry posted the truck for sale online and taped a sign to the front window before heading out for work. The sign said: FOR SALE $14,000. He chose the price because that was about how much he owed on the loan, plus, that's about how much he figured it was worth. In the coming weeks, he got a couple of interested buyers making low-ball offers. Eventually, a guy came around who wasn't looking to haggle, and took the truck off Larry's hands for the asking price.

Larry's Lawn Care was back down to one truck and one guy, but there were still about 70 clients to deal with. As spring came around, Larry made sure everyone knew he was taking no more work. He wasn't going to do any estimates for any new jobs, period. The phone was ringing constantly, and he had to explain this to everyone that called. Getting tired of dealing with it, Larry decided just to automate his rejections. He changed his voicemail to a generic message that told all callers that Larry's Lawn Care was maxed out, and could take no new work.

When March hit, Larry was like a workhorse, constantly pushing a mower. He wasn't sleeping much, wasn't eating much, and always on the move. He had slightly fewer customers, down to about 60. To fit in all the work he had scheduled, he was at full tilt, working almost 80 hour weeks. All of the work was really paying off though — he was pulling in a total of $10,000 a month.

Without paying for employees, gas for a second truck or payments on it, Larry got to keep a lot of the money he made… even with the monthly IRS payment. He was in full control of the work too, so his customers were always happy. Every time he mowed a tough corner on an old customer's property, he was reminded of a time last fall when Marvin missed it entirely, causing Larry to do it himself. Each time he mowed a client's lawn, he noticed the little extra touches he made, reinforcing his belief that employees were a terrible mistake.

To maintain his constant work schedule, Larry got really good at managing his time. He became super efficient, packing his days with jobs from dawn to dusk, not leaving much time for eating breakfast, lunch and dinner. Getting into a rhythm, it became the new routine. The grind was rough though, and chipping away at Larry's health.

Larry's late work nights caused him to miss dinner all the time. Savannah began saving his portions, hoping he would eat when he got home. She wasn't able to make sure he did, since she was often putting James to sleep when Larry would walk into the apartment. By the time James was down for the night, Larry would have showered and crashed on the bed, snoring. He typically would eat what was saved the following day for lunch. Savannah began noticing bags under Larry's eyes, and saw that his arms and legs were becoming more lean.

Though she really liked the new stability his hard work was bringing the family — all the money was really great — she became worried it wasn't sustainable. Larry was physically drained, and he hardly got to spend any time just enjoying the family. She couldn't remember that last time he read James a story, or played with him, or spent time alone with him. Later in the summer, things started to get worse.

Larry woke up one morning in June with pain in his throat. He was freezing, but his body felt hot to the touch. Thinking he could soothe his throat and warm himself up with some tea, he put some hot water on and steeped some. Sipping it calmed his throat for moments at a time, but the pain was pretty intense. Savannah was sure Larry had strep throat, and urged him to see a doctor.

"I'm fine, I don't need a doctor," he said, brushing it off.

"Larry, I think you have a fever... you can't work with a fever," Savannah said. "Let's take your temperature, and if I'm right, go see a doctor, OK?"

"Maybe," he said.

Savannah brought out the thermometer and Larry held it in his mouth beneath his tongue until it started beeping. Looking at the instrument, it read 98.8℉. Larry thought this was no big deal, but Savannah thought it proved her point.

"It's an old thermometer, and it only showed that I'm only .2℉ higher than I should be. That's not enough to waste a day at the doctor's office. I have a lot of work to do," he said.

Concerned, but realizing he was too stubborn to budge, Savannah let him go to work.

Larry got into the truck, shivering even though the heat of the summer sun had made the black leather seats hot. Starting it up, he headed to his first mow job of the day. On the road, he began coughing, each one more painful than the next. *"It's just a cold,"* he told himself.

Arriving at the property, he pulled out the mower and got to work. He was push mowing most of the day. It was more difficult than usual, and his legs and arms felt fatigued by noon, but Larry pushed on undeterred. He could still smell the fresh cut grass, which he took as a sign that his cold wasn't that bad afterall. When he got home, Savannah had homemade chicken noodle soup ready for him. James was put to bed early, because she needed to make sure Larry ate dinner that night. The soup was delicious, and numbed his throat pain a bit.

The next morning, Larry could hardly swallow the pain was so great. He was sore throughout his entire body, and had trouble talking. Savannah was awake just as early as he was today, concerned about his sickness. It was tough for her to see him struggling so hard to get out of bed and start the day. She did as much as she could to help him, preparing breakfast and helping get the equipment ready.

"Larry," she said, hesitating a bit. "I think it's time to find someone else to help do the work."

"Absolutely not," he said defiantly. "We just went through this, I don't need a repeat of last year."

"You can find one good employee, and pay them a bit more this time," she said. "We are making plenty of money right now, we can take a cut on the profit side and be absolutely fine."

"No, Savannah, that's not on the table," he said. "This is the best the business has done since it started. We are making plenty of money, I am in full control, nothing has been broken, and all of my customers are happy. I can't go backwards."

"Well, something will have to change. It's too much on you," she said. "I'll keep thinking of what we can do. You should think about it too."

With that, he headed out to work.

The day was an absolute trial to get through. He didn't know what was wrong, he had never felt this ill before, but he had to work. There was just no getting around it. Larry pushed his hardest to get through the day, with the loud humming of the mower in the background. He thought about his wife and son, and how little he gets to see them, feeling a bit trapped in his current situation. He was constantly working because he had to, and he couldn't stop.

Feeling the intensity of the pain in his throat, he feared illness would become more common for him. He knew his body was run down, and his immune system wasn't as strong as it had been. *"What if I keep getting sick all the time…"* he thought, feeling a whirlwind of anxiety hit. Then his concerns about his family jumped into the fray. *"What if my son grows up without me? What if I can't handle having a second child in the future?"* his heart was beating faster than normal, but he pushed on.

Calming himself down, he thought about the positives of his business. He thought about how much money he was making, and how loyal his clients were. He reminded himself that the quality of his work was better than the competition. *"I just need to toughen up,"* he thought.

He wasn't as quick as usual, so he finished the day later. On the way home, absolutely beat, he stopped at a gas station to refill the truck. He was sweaty and shaky as he hopped out of the driver's seat to grab the fuel nozzle. In front of him, he noticed a familiar truck — it was older, looked a bit beat up, and connected to a trailer full of lawn care equipment. He walked inside the gas station to prepay for his fuel, when he noticed a very frustrated looking Pedro in the snack aisle.

"No way, Pedro, what's up!" Larry said, walking up to him to give him a hug.

Pedro's eyes lit up when he saw him. "Oh my gosh, dude, how's life?" he said, embracing Larry. They hadn't talked since Larry quit working for Joe.

"It's good man, I'm making good money, I have good clients," he said. "I'm kinda sick right now, but otherwise it's great."

"And the kid? How's Savannah?" Pedro asked.

"My son is great. His name is James, he's a smart healthy kid. Savannah is doing great too, she quit working and is a full-time mom now," Larry said, smiling.

They got in line together to pay, and caught up on each others lives. Pedro bought a bag of chips to snack on, and they both paid for their gas. Leaving the station and walking towards their trucks, Larry asked more questions.

"How's working for Joe?" he said.

Pedro rolled his eyes. "Just as terrible. I'm kinda over it. My wages haven't changed, and he won't promote me at all. His equipment just keeps getting worse too — he never buys new stuff." Pedro glanced over at Larry's truck. "I would much rather be driving that thing around," he said, gesturing to it.

"Yeah, it is pretty nice," he said laughing, but then a cough escaped him. He covered his mouth and tried not to show how painful it was.

"The other thing is, I work with Ben all the time. Ben has gotten better at stuff, but I really just don't like working with him," Pedro said. "Joe likes him quite a bit though."

Larry, tired and not really thinking the idea through, blurted out something that all of a sudden seemed like a good idea.

"Bro, come work for me, I'll give you $15 an hour!" he said. "But you gotta start tomorrow."

Pedro looked over at Larry's truck again, and just like that, he sealed the deal.

"That sounds great! I'll be at your place tomorrow morning!" he said, shaking Larry's hand.

"Great, see you then," Larry said, getting back into his truck. *"Oh God, what did I just do...I just went through all this garbage,"* he thought to himself. However, he knew Savannah would be happy about it. And he knew Pedro was a good worker, because he had worked with him before. *"He's going to reduce my workload... that way I can be with my family and not wear out my body,"* he thought. He was almost home at this point. *"And like Savannah said, we can afford to lose some profit... I'll be making a similar amount of money."* Feeling more confident, but still unsure, he told himself he would keep a handle on it this time.

It was pretty late when he pulled into his driveway, and walked upstairs into the apartment. Each step was more difficult than the first. Exhausted, he showered and crawled into bed. Savannah woke up.

"How are you feeling?" she whispered, half awake.

"I'm feeling.... Okay," he said, quickly falling asleep.

That morning, Pedro showed up just like he said he would. Larry, still sick, worked with him throughout the morning, trying his best to hide the cough. But Pedro noticed it by 10 a.m.

"Larry, why don't you go see a doctor tomorrow," he said. "You sound really sick. I can cover your jobs for you, you know that."

Larry thought about it for a second, but he knew Pedro was right. He had let himself remain sick for too long, and was getting concerned himself.

"Yeah, you're right. Savannah has been telling me to go," he said. "Keep me posted all day though."

When he finally went to the doctor, he was diagnosed with strep throat. His fever was worse too, but still low-grade and below 100℉. The doctor scolded him for not seeing him sooner, and put him on ten days of antibiotics. He told him to rest for a day, but that he could go back to work within 24 hours. Larry decided just to take the remainder of the day off and go back to work tomorrow.

Things started to get better while working with Pedro. He still had a consistent client base of happy customers, and they worked well together, just like old times. Pedro loved working with Larry, and Larry loved working with Pedro. They were able to take on a couple new jobs, but Larry made sure not to overdo it. All throughout July, Larry was able to take Saturdays off. He started doing fun things with the family each weekend — one weekend they went to the zoo, another they went swimming, and they went out for dinner for the first time in months.

One night, they were reading a book with James, when Savannah started to a feel a little bit sick. She drank some water, trying to calm her stomach. The feeling was familiar — she had felt this way before.

"Larry, I am going to pick up some medicine at the store, I'll be right pack," she said quietly. "You guys finish the book without me."

He nodded and gave her a kiss.

Savannah grabbed some nausea medication, but decided to pick up a pregnancy test too, just in case. When she returned home, Larry had finished reading the book and had tucked James in bed.

Once Larry got into bed, she revealed the news. She was pregnant. This time, he was not nervous or worried at all. Larry was excited, and he was ready to build the family. They were more stable than he had ever been. They fell asleep together feeling good about the future.

The following week was the first week of August. Pedro and Larry were both in good spirits, even though it was a long week with more work than usual. They had a couple of one-time jobs sprinkled in with their recurring mows. Finishing up the week on Friday, they were both relieved and ready for the weekend. They joked around in the truck on the way back to Larry's place, both of them covered in dirt and grass, ready to be done for the day.

Larry was driving about 40 miles per hour, Pedro had turned up the music, and was leaning back in his chair. Larry wasn't wearing his seatbelt — it was a short drive to his apartment from their last job. They were bantering back and forth like brothers, reliving some of the days setbacks and accomplishments. Larry saw they were approaching a familiar intersection near his place, and sighed with relief.

"The final stretch," he said.

Their truck entered the intersection, and all of a sudden, Larry's memory went black. Another truck had pulled into the intersection at the same speed, running right through a red light and into the driver's side of Larry's truck. The impact rendered Larry unconscious, and his body went limp as it shot straight forward and crashed through the passenger side of the windshield; flying over Pedro, through glass and hitting pavement.

His body was motionless in the middle of the street. After a couple of seconds, he began to flutter in and out of consciousness. Larry opened his eyes to see shards of glass laying scattered in front of him, glistening in the evening sun. A small pool of blood was crawling toward it. Fear struck Larry's heart and forced his body into motion — he tried to stand, but he couldn't move his legs. Shakily pushing his torso up with his arms, he turned his head to look behind him, and saw Pedro unconscious in the passenger seat of the truck. The metal on the front end of the other truck, still in the same position of impact, was crumpled into itself like a wad of paper.

That was the last thing he remembered before fainting back onto the ground. The next thing Larry knew, he was waking up in the hospital.

CHAPTER 5: THE BUSINESS ON LIFE-SUPPORT

Larry slowly opened his eyes, waking up after a deep, dreamless sleep. He saw Savannah sitting in a chair next to him, and she noticed he was awake. Leaning forward, she grabbed his hand and kissed him on the forehead.

"How are you feeling?" she asked.

Larry leaned up in the bed, realizing where he was. They were in a hospital room. His memory started flooding back to him — the impact of the truck, his immobile legs, the broken glass shards by his face — then he remembered seeing Pedro unconscious in the passenger seat.

"Is Pedro okay?" Larry asked frantically.

"Yes, Pedro is okay now. He was sent home," Savannah said. "However, you have a few days to go before you can leave."

She began explaining to Larry in detail what had happened in the crash. He remembered it pretty vividly as she rehashed the details. He began to feel stinging pains along his face and arms, gasping a bit at the pain.

"Yeah, that's the road rash," Savannah said.

Just then, a doctor entered the room holding a clipboard.

"Larry, I'm glad to see you're awake," she said. "I gotta tell you, you are extremely lucky to be conscious.

That was a really close call, but you managed to escape with some bad road rash and small fractures."

His body was limp when he ejected from the vehicle, and he happened to land on the ground in a way that protected his head, she explained. The brunt of the impact was on his left arm, which had a hairline fracture and fairly deep abrasions. He had lost a lot of blood, which caused him to faint at the scene.

"What about my legs?" Larry asked. "I couldn't move them after the crash."

"Well, can you feel them now?" the doctor asked.

Larry focused on his legs and feet, wiggling his toes and sighing in relief when he realized he could move them.

"The shock probably made you weak," the doctor assured him. "You're legs are going to be just fine."

She told Larry and Savannah that he would need to stay in the hospital so they could monitor him for a few more days, and that once he was released, he would need between two and three more weeks of rest at least. She told them to watch for infection, and to stock up on gauze so he could keep his many abrasions covered. The wound dressings would need to be replaced at least once a day.

After the doctor left the room, Larry started worrying about how expensive his hospital stay would be. He remembered how long it took to pay off the medical debt from Savannah giving birth to James, and hoped the bill wouldn't be as high as that. Especially considering the fact that he was out of work for a few weeks. Thinking of Pedro, Larry felt terrible. *"I don't know if he has any insurance..."* Larry thought to himself. Pedro was working under the table.

Then, he thought about the ramifications for his business. *"Oh my gosh... I'm going to lose all my customers,"* he thought. Larry could feel the weight of his life crashing down on him. He was going to have to formulate a plan for damage control — for his body, his business and his finances. With both Larry and Pedro out of commission, there was no one to do the work, and if he didn't figure out something fast... Larry knew he would be swamped with debt, and have no income to pay for it.

Realizing he was stuck, Larry saw only one way out. He would have to sell his business. If he could get a good amount of money for it, he could pay his bills and his customers would be taken care of. He turned to Savannah, who was still sitting next to him and holding his hand.

"Babe, do you know where my phone is?" Larry asked.

Savannah was hesitant. "Yes... I have it. Here you go."

When she handed it to him, the screen lit up, and he could see immediately that it was full of messages — emails, missed phone calls, texts — which only solidified his decision. Larry thought about the other lawn care businesses in the area, and knew just who to call. The company that seemed the most capable of buying a business was Parscapes. They had great employees, equipment, and from what Larry had heard around town, they did a great job.

Savannah left the hospital to tend to James at home, who was being babysat by a friend. She kissed Larry goodbye, and said she would see him again tomorrow. After she left, Larry searched online for Parscapes, found the company phone number, and called, asking for the owner. The guy's name was Phil. The company had a receptionist, who transferred Larry's call to Phil. When he picked up the phone, Larry introduced himself, and they chatted for a bit. After the small talk, Larry got down to the issue.

"Phil, I have a problem," he said. "I got into a car accident, and my only employee was in the car with me. We are both unable to work for a while. I won't be able to get out into the field again for a few weeks. I think I have a solution that we can both benefit from."

"I'm sorry to hear that, Larry. What are you thinking?" Phil asked, intrigued.

"I know Parscapes is a successful company, and I think you guys would do a better job taking care of my customers. I think you should buy my business from me," Larry said.

The phone was quiet for a second, and then Larry heard Phil sigh. "Well, Larry, I'm not sure if we will be able to buy your business. However, I do think we might be able to sort something out. I realize the issue is time sensitive, because you have customers who need service.

Why don't I drop by the hospital this evening and we can talk?"

Surprised, Larry agreed.

After the sun went down, Phil showed up at Larry's hospital room. Seeing him in person, Larry was both excited and nervous. He ran some numbers in his head, trying to decide how much he could sell his business for. *"I could sell my business for $250,000, and that would help me pay off my debts and put money in the bank for the next baby… maybe even a downpayment for a house,"* he thought. *"Then I could just work for Phil."* Walking into the room, Phil walked over to Larry's bed and they shook hands. Phil sat down in the seat that Savannah had used earlier that day.

"Ok, let's get down to business," Larry said. "Buy me out now, and I'll work for you when I've healed up."

Phil scratched his head. "Larry, that might not work for us. We are already growing a lot. It kinda depends on how much you want to sell the business for. We could only do, like, $30,000 to $40,000 or so," Phil said. "I know that's probably not what you want to hear."

Larry's heart dropped to his stomach. This was his only hope. He started to get angry at what he felt was a low-ball offer. Larry had built his business with grit, determination and hard work. *"How could he say my business is only worth $30,000?"* he thought. Phil noticed his frustration and tried to explain.

"Hey, with you gone, the business isn't worth much. There's no valuable systems and procedures, and your customers are connected to you as a person rather than your brand. If you leave, they probably won't stick around" Phil said. "However, I do think we can help you. I'm willing to take on your clients until you are back on your feet."

Astonished at the offer, Larry perked up a bit.

"At this point, you I don't think you should sell your business," Phil continued. "You should keep working on it. It's not really worth anything to an outside buyer at this point. It's barely worth the value of your equipment."

"Well, if you would maintain my clients for me, that would definitely help…" Larry said. Phil nodded in agreement. Larry couldn't believe a competitor would help keep his business afloat.

"We'll take care of the mowing and when you are feeling better you can just continue on," Phil said. With that, they exchanged pleasantries and said goodbye.

Once Larry was alone in the hospital room, he contemplated what Phil told him. His business had no systems, no procedures, and hardly any value. All of his hard work had procured him a business that was worth a fraction of the revenue it was pulling in. He thought about systems, and what Phil meant by that…then he started to put it together.

Larry remembered when he first started the business, and how he went about hiring his first employees. There was no consistency to his interview process, and he didn't really vet his employees well, which resulted in him firing them both the same year. Larry started to realize there were plenty of other examples he could think of that reflected what Phil meant. He thought back to the time when he saw a Parscapes crew working efficiently and professionally on a property, and realized he had been doing everything wrong. *"If I'm going to keep running this business, I need Phil's help,"* he realized. *"If I don't have guidance, this whole thing is just going to become a cycle."*

Larry slept through the night, but his sleep was troubled. The next morning, he reluctantly called Phil again. Sucking up his pride, he was honest with Phil, his competitor, admitting he needed help.

"I admire what you've built," Larry said. "If I can, I'd like to learn from you how to build a successful business."

Phil was empathetic, and he agreed to help. Larry was blown away. "You should be resting, so I'll come see you at the hospital. I can visit for an hour or so each day for the next few days," Phil said.

After Phil agreed to help, Larry was hopeful. He imagined his business flourishing, but he could still see it potentially failing. He felt like he was standing on the precipice of success and failure. The more he examined his own role in the instability his business has constantly felt, the more he realized he had set himself up to fail, but hoped that Phil could help him pursue success.

When Phil arrived that evening, Larry felt broken. He knew he hadn't built a valuable business, and he was embarrassed that he had thought it was worth hundreds of thousands of dollars only the day prior. He was about to admit to his competitor that he had failed, and that was painful to do. Phil sat down again in the same chair he had the day before, and Larry couldn't look him in the eye.

"How are you feeling today?" Phil asked.

It took a moment for Larry to respond. His emotions were getting the better of him. He felt small and weak, and he felt sorry for his family and the people he had hired. He felt sorry for himself, too.

"You were right," Larry said. "Without me, my business is nothing. I can't believe I couldn't see that." Thinking about James, he started to well up, but he tried his best to hold back tears — he didn't want to cry in front of this stranger, let alone a man who had accomplished everything Larry had set out to do. "It's my dream to be able to build a strong business. When I started this, I thought that's what I was doing. I wanted this business to make the kind of money that could pay for my son's college tuition. I even wanted to be able to pass down the business to him one day. I just don't know how to do it, but I thought I did."

A nurse entered the room to check on Larry, and asked if he needed anything. He said he was fine, but thanked her. As she left, he turned back to Phil.

"I'm great at doing lawn care and landscaping, but I'm not good at business," he admitted. "I can't believe you're willing to help me, even though I'm a competing business owner," he said.

Phil smiled. "There's tons of work out there. I don't look at you as competition. A rising tide floats all boats higher. I'm happy to help."

That reasoning made Larry feel less like a charity case. Phil was the perfect mentor — he didn't look down on Larry, which made him more comfortable. He felt like it was okay to ask for his help.

"Well, what's the secret? How do you do it?" he asked.

"There isn't a magic bullet," Phil said. "At the end of the day, it's still a lot of work. But the work is ON you as a person, rather than out in the business. You're still gonna work hard, you're not gonna work less, but the work is going to be different."

"What do you mean?" Larry asked.

"The first thing you have to do is build a team," Phil said.

Phil explained the concept to Larry in detail. A solid team is important for the business and the employer. Owners need to have a strong team, so that when they are sick, or injured or get hit by a truck, they can rely on their employees to run the business. Besides that, having a team creates the foundation for a business model that is profitable, and scalable. If the weight and responsibility of the work rests only on the business owner, the business can't grow — it becomes limited to what one person is capable of. If you want to make more money, you need to have a strong team.

"Nothing great was ever created by one person," Phil said.

Larry was perplexed by this statement. "What about people like Martin Luther King? He started the civil rights movement."

"Yes, he did spearhead a movement. But was he the one guy who caused the change? Or did he get lots of other people to join him in the fight for civil rights?"

Larry pondered for a second, realizing what Phil was trying to say.

When it comes to starting a business, the owner has to be a leader who gets a group of people behind his or her idea. Then, the owner has to delegate responsibilities to other people. The owner has to let go of total control, and has to place a certain amount of trust in other people, realizing that they probably won't do the job exactly the way they want it done 100 percent of the time.

Phil acknowledged that it's hard to let go of the control over your business. It's difficult to let other people do a job that you know you can do better. However, he likened this mentality to authoritarianism. When all control is centralized in one individual, it's not sustainable. He told Larry to think about the Roman Empire, and how Roman dictators contributed to instability and the eventual fall of the empire. Everyone has flaws and gaps in competence that need to be filled by other people, he said.

"If you are always the one making all the decisions, eventually you will make a wrong decision," Phil said. "Looking back at the dictators of history, their empires have fallen — the rulers couldn't be criticized, challenged or second guessed. That's what leads to demise. You want to foster a culture where your team can share their opinions and ideas that will make the business better and offer a different perspective than your own. For us at Parscapes, some of our best innovations and ideas have come from our front-line employees."

Additionally, business owners have to step away from the work itself. As a lawn care business owner, this means getting out of the fields, Phil explained. For the business to run well, the owner has to be like a football head coach, rather than the star player. Even though the owner has the resources and ability to play the game better than everyone else, he has to step out of the field and onto the sideline. The business owner has to be the strategist.

"When you know you could do a better job as the quarterback, or the running back or the wide receiver, you still have to step back because you can't be the entire team," Phil said. "You need all the pieces of the team together. Get off the field and allow the team to play their role! Everyone has a position and role that makes the team strong."

From a business standpoint, having a team is more profitable, more safe, and more scalable. From an employer standpoint, there's things that have to be worked on, like humility, and being able to create a culture and environment where people want to work. Having humility is a big deal — most employers in the landscape industry can't build a team because they're not humble enough to admit when they're wrong, or allow for open criticism of themselves, or admit that they can't do everything within the business. It's the job of the owner to create an environment where there can be constructive criticism, where people can learn from each other

"Creating that team that has a solid connection between the head coach and the players, where the players respect the head coach for his strategic abilities, and the coach realizes that he cannot step on the field and actually do the work," Phil said. "You need to realize that that is your role — the head coach."

Phil stressed that one role is not better than the other, and no role is lesser than the other. It's just about finding people to operate at their highest capabilities in their role within the business.

To use the analogy of a football team, the wide receiver shouldn't judge the linebacker for being fat and slow. The linebacker has traits and strengths that allow him to perform best in HIS position of linebacker. The linebacker shouldn't judge the wide receiver for not being able to bench press 300 pounds. The receiver's position requires him to be lean, quick, and light. The same is true for a business. The office person that has strengths of marketing, calling customers, and closing sales should never devalue the importance of the laborers mowing lawns and trimming trees… and vice versa. The team is greater than the sum of all its parts.

It was getting late, and their conversation had drawn to an end. Larry looked at his arms, bound in gauze, and realized that his business would have been resilient if he had built a team when he hired his first two guys. Getting into a car accident wouldn't have struck fear into him about losing all his customers if he had a team to take care of the business. He wouldn't be needing Phils help — he could have relied on the strength of his team and his coaching staff.

CHAPTER 6: CREATING A SYSTEMS-CENTRIC BUSINESS

The next morning, Larry woke up unusually early. It was his third day in the hospital. Late summer sun was streaming in through the hospital window, peeking through the curtains and making its way to the foot of Larry's hospital bed. He was antsy, and not used to laying in bed so much. He stretched out and slowly got up, trying not to put weight on his arms. Once he was on his feet, he stood for a moment, leaning on the side of the bed. His legs ached from bruises, and movement rubbed against his scrapes, occasionally causing stinging pains. He slowly walked to the window and looked out, then returned to his bed and laid back down.

He checked his phone, and saw Phil left him a voicemail. He would head over to visit Larry later that morning. Sighing, Larry figured he would be alone in bed for a couple of hours. He couldn't wait to talk to Phil again. Larry called in a nurse to let them know he was ready to eat, and later a man showed up with a tray of oatmeal, fruit, milk and water. He picked at his breakfast slowly while thinking about his business. Phil arrived a short time later, while Larry was finishing his meal.

In his hand, Phil was carrying a book. "I figured you might like to read this when you have nothing else to do," he said. "It's called *The E-Myth*, written by Michael

Gerber. Every entrepreneur should read this book to get the base knowledge of systems and procedures."

Larry took the book from Phil's hand. "Thanks, Phil."

Phil sat down and leaned back in his chair. "There needs to be systems and procedures with everything you do within your business. The closer you can get it to being thus, the less the business is reliant on you as a person."

He talked about how entrepreneurs are often capable of building a business off of their personalities, but that it costs them in the long run. Building a business on the personality of one person is like creating a foundation on one strong pillar. If you build one massive pillar, you can build a pretty good structure on top of it — but when the entrepreneur is taken away from that business, the structure falls.

If you're going to construct a large building such as a giant condominium structure, there has to be multiple smaller pillars throughout the foundation. Systems and procedures are the many small pillars that hold up a business, and prevent the structure from crumbling if the entrepreneur is knocked out from the foundation. Entrepreneurs need to ask themselves what they are building their businesses on.

"The goal and objective is to make a systems-centric business, rather than a personality-centric business," Phil said.

Larry set his breakfast tray down on a desk next to him on the other side of his bed, and sat up to listen. "I need some concrete examples of this," he said. "I don't really get what you mean, but I know you said that my business was lacking these things... therefore not worth much."

"Right. Of course," he said. "When it comes to a lawn care business, there has to be a process for everything from routing, to scheduling, to billing, to estimating, to invoicing, to hiring, to firing and how the business responds to issues from a human resources standpoint."

"So what kind of system would be associated with, say, estimates?" Larry asked.

"When you get a phone call from a new, potential customer, there should be a system that the customer is pumped through — starting with how you answer the phone," he said. "Answering the phone should be done the same way, every single time, and there should be no guesswork involved."

Phil explained that the next step in the estimate process is scheduling the appointment for the estimator to look at the job. When scheduling, does the customer get a time slot of an hour? Do you book them same day? Do you book them tomorrow? Phil explained that there are tons of variables, but that a system helps manage the variables.

Second, once the estimator shows up to the property, there should be a system for the interaction. Does the estimator hand the customer an informational packet? When do they give them that information? Before, during or after seeing the job? There should also be a process for closing the meeting, as well — for instance, if the office is going to get back to the customer about the estimate, will it be within 24 hours or 48 hours? Will the estimate be emailed or printed?

Once the customer hopefully accepts the estimate, there should be another process. Is the customer put on the schedule the next day, or the next week? How is that determined? Do they need to provide a down payment? If so, when is that required — for everything from $10 job to a $10,000 job, or just the $10,000 job? Is it 25 percent or 50 percent up front? Every step of the process should have answers to these questions, which creates the system and procedures team members follow.

"How long does it take to create all those systems and procedures?" Larry asked.

"There is no finish line, because the system can always be improved," Phil explained. "The process of creating systems and procedures has to continually evolve."

From a financial standpoint, having systems and procedures makes a business more efficient. It also is better for customers, because they can expect the same treatment no matter who in the business they are working with. Employees come and go, but if the business is built on systems, everything becomes more consistent, including customer service. Additionally, whoever is working creates the same product every time, because the system creates the product rather than the people.

"Whatever the system is, there's no right or wrong," Phil said. "You just need a framework as a starting point that you can continue to work on."

A nurse walked in and took Larry's breakfast tray from the table it was sitting on. Larry thanked her and asked for a glass of water, and she returned within a few minutes with a clear plastic cup filled to the brim. Larry took a sip, and thought about the systems that the nurse follows. *"I wonder how many systems are being implemented while she does her job,"* he thought.

"I bet that's plenty for you to chew on for now," Phil said. "I gotta get going, but seriously, I think you'll get a lot out of that book."

Larry shook Phil's hand, thanking him again for his help. It was midday by now, and Savannah was heading over to visit for lunch. She brought him a sandwich and soup from a local deli, and they hung out for a couple hours in his room. As they flipped through magazines, Larry filled Savannah in about what he was learning from Phil, and Savannah filled Larry in on how things were going at home. They talked about James. Then, Savannah went home to relieve the babysitter.

Larry took a nap that afternoon. When he woke up, he picked up the book that Phil brought him, and cracked it open. He wasn't much of a reader, but if the book could help him revive his business, he was highly interested. It turned out to be quite the page-turner for

Larry, and by late that evening, he had gotten half way through it. Larry went to bed with a number of new concepts floating around in his head, and woke up the following morning ready to learn more.

Phil arrived at the hospital room around the same time the following morning, Larry's fourth day of recovery. He gave Larry an update on how his customers were fairing without him.

"You're customers miss you, that's for sure," Phil said, chuckling. "But everything is going great. No complaints. A few of them have been asking how you're doing."

Larry smiled. His customers were definitely loyal to him, but would they like the new systems-centric business we was concocting in his mind?

They chatted for a bit, and Phil offered to grab them both some coffee from the cafeteria. He left, and Larry picked up *The E-Myth* again to catch up where he left off. When Phil came back clutching two coffees in his hands, Larry set the book back down.

"Looks like you've gotten pretty far," Phil said. "Have you learned much yet?"

"Yeah, I see myself a lot in this story as I read it," he said. "Once I finish, I'll tell you more."

"Good. Well, I've got some more business tips for you today," Phil said. "So far, we've talked about the importance of building a team and having systems, but there's more to it than that. All the things I'm talking to you about are interconnected, and without one of them, the whole company isn't going to reach the full extent of its potential."

If your business has a great team, but not a great system, you're not going to create a consistent result. If the business has great systems but doesn't have a great team, there will be a lot of turnover and instability, making the systems ineffective.

"The third thing I want to talk to you about is numbers," Phil said. "To have a successful business, you gotta know your numbers. Your absolutely MUST know your numbers!"

When you know your numbers, you know if the consistent result that your team and your systems are producing is effective for your business. You can determine how much it costs for your team to run your systems, and compare that cost to the income it brings in. Additionally, you can find out how satisfied your customers are with what you produce, and use these objective standards to tweak your systems and your team.

"If you don't know your numbers, you can't tweak the system and you can't make changes within the team to make a better, more consistent product for your customer," Phil said.

The owner needs to know the basics: revenue per month, revenue per week and revenue per day. They also need to know what their overhead costs are, and what their fixed costs are versus their variable costs. Overhead costs are the costs associated with operating the business, such as insurance, licensing, and office staff. Fixed costs are things that don't change, even when the company gets more business — these might include your equipment loans and shop rent. Variable costs are the costs that change according to the amount of business you generate, with the biggest ones being labor expense and material costs.

"This is really important stuff to know, especially when you're just starting out," Phil said. "You need to know how much money you need to make in a month to cover those fixed costs, and cover your variable costs. Basically, you need to know how much revenue you need to bring in each month to break-even."

Diving a little deeper, there are a many other numbers that owners need to have on hand. When it comes to landscaping, some of the most important numbers to know have to do with customers. Landscape and lawn care business owners need to know how much it costs to bring in a new customer, and how much that customer is worth to the company in the long run. These figures are known as the Customer Acquisition Cost (CAC), and the Customer Lifetime Value (CLV).

When determining the cost of customer acquisition, a business owner must take into account the amount they are spending on generating leads and reeling in that new customer. Often, these costs come from advertising. For example, if an owner uses pay-per-click online advertisements, it might cost $10 to get a potential customer to click, but it may also take at least five clicks to generate an actual lead that contacts your business.

The cost jumps up to $50 per lead at that point. After that, how many leads does it take to create an estimate? And how many estimates does it take to create a job? Then, what's the value of that job? The profit on that job better be more than the cost it takes to get the clicks, which become leads, which becomes estimates, which turn into paying customers. Reducing the friction along that path of clicking to a paying customer is important to keep consumers inside of your sales funnel.

Overall, the customer acquisition cost takes into account the whole process, from the first click to then sending out estimates and offering proposals, to then producing the job. At the end of the day, there's a profit margin. Does that cover your Customer Acquisition Cost? To find out how much a customer is worth to the business over their entire lifetime, the owner needs to know the average lifespan of their customers. Is it two years? Is it three years? Is it a one-time buy?

"The value of your jobs better equate to a whole lot more than what you paid to acquire that customer," Phil said. "For instance, typically at Parscapes if we put $100 into online advertising, we get ten leads. Out of those ten leads, we get two jobs, and those two jobs may be worth around $2,000. The average customer will buy that service 3 times over the course of 3 years. This results in a Customer Lifetime Value of $6,000."

Then, there are a whole lot of numbers associated with the crew. The owner needs to know the efficiency numbers of a job based on how many people are there —

for instance, the costs of sending a one man crew, vs. a two man or a three man crew. What's the dollars of income produced per hour of labor? Additionally, what's the profitability of different types of services? When that information is put together, the owner can determine what the profit margins are for each type of job.

"You need to know what your most profitable service is, and also what your least profitable one is," Phil said.

Larry sighed, feeling a bit overwhelmed. "This is so much Phil — I don't know most of these numbers when it comes to my business. I have a pretty good idea of how much revenue I am bringing in, and how much profit I typically take home. But I have no idea how much I am spending on my customers and my crew... let alone all the other stuff."

Phil laughed. "I figured. That's why I'm telling you. It won't be easy turning around your business but it's the only way to build the kind of business you've dreamed of."

He stood up and got ready to leave, picking up their empty coffee cups so he could throw them away. Larry was a little bit bummed. *"I have so many questions still,"* he thought.

"Phil, I don't know how I can do all of this," he said, starting to panic a bit. "There's so much I didn't think about, so much I didn't realize when I started..."

Phil tossed the cups into a small waste basket next to the hospital room door, and turned back to respond.

"You're not gonna figure this all out today," he said. "Just keep learning, and you'll get it."

CHAPTER 7: BUILDING A BRAND

Savannah came to visit Larry early in the morning his last day at the hospital. Larry was feeling stronger, and his abrasions were healing up well. He was able to move more freely without as much pain. Excited to get out of the hospital room and back home, Larry was energetic. Sitting next to him, Savannah gave him a kiss on the cheek and smiled.

"James is excited to see you come home," she said.

"I'm excited to be home," Larry said, leaning back and sighing. "It's horrible being stuck in this room all of the time. I've also been learning so much, and I can't wait to start putting my knowledge to use."

"Tell me about it," Savannah said. "I know Phil has been teaching you a lot, but you've only told me a little bit about it. What's the most important thing you've learned?"

Larry scratched his chin and gave the question a bit of thought before giving her an answer.

"You know, I have learned a lot from Phil — mostly about all of the mistakes I made when I started the business," he said, getting a little red in the face from embarrassment. "What's fresh in my mind is actually from a book he gave me that I've been reading. I just finished it."

Larry picked up *The E-Myth* from the table next to him and handed it to Savannah.

"I was glued to it all night. I learned some stuff about myself that I think will improve my business," he told her. "For instance, the book described something called an entrepreneurial seizure. I remember the moment I decided to start my business, and how it changed the way I viewed…. Everything."

Savannah laughed. "I remember that too."

"And it also described something I have felt for so long now, but never really knew how to put words to. The writer said lots of entrepreneurs start as great technicians — they are good at doing the work they do, and they take pride in it. Like how I am with mowing," he said. "But when you become a business owner, you have to remove yourself from the role of a technician, to the role of a manager, which is a totally different thing. It's like the technician and the manager within me have been fighting throughout the growth of my business."

Savannah looked a bit confused, like she sort of understood what he was saying, but was not fully on the same page.

"I think you would have to read the book to understand what I mean," Larry said.

They sat and chatted for a while longer before Savannah had to get back home. She told Larry she would be back to pick him up that evening. Larry missed her when she left, more than usual, probably because he was antsy to get home.

When Phil arrived that morning, Larry was excited to to pick up where they left off. He stood up from the hospital bed this time to greet Phil at the door as he was walking down the hallway. Larry peaked his head out and waved at him, and Phil picked up his pace, meeting up with Larry at the doorway.

"Woah, woah! Sit back down, Larry, you aren't totally healed yet," Phil said, chuckling and leading him back to the bed inside the room. "You do look pretty good today though."

Larry sat down on the edge of the bed, but refused to lay down. He leaned forward with his elbows on his knees so he was at about the same level as Phil when he sat down in the chair next to him.

"I finished the book," Larry said smiling. "I'm ready to hear what advice you have for me today. Tonight I'm gonna be leaving."

Larry handed Phil *The E-Myth*, and he set it down on his lap. "Alright Larry, if you're ready then I'm ready," he said.

"I have some specific questions actually. I know I need to build a team and create systems and that I need to know my numbers, and that's all fine and good, but... how do I actually grow my business?" Larry asked. "How do I generate leads, and keep busy, but grow sustainably? If I'm going to have a team and grow sustainably, I probably need to get to a million dollars a year in revenue... and that just seems so out of reach. I grew my little business quickly but mostly just through some flyers and word-of-mouth."

"The thing that's going to answer that is sales," Phil said. "However, we need to have a conversation about branding before we talk about sales."

If you want to sell your business one day, you have to create a valuable brand as well as sell to consumers, he explained. Branding is the long term game. It takes a lot of work that doesn't pay off immediately, but it's really important to start early. When you go to sell your business in the future, the brand is where the real value lies. It is the logo recognition, the customer trust, and all of the intangible assets of a business that's left when you strip away the equipment, like trucks, trailers and lawn mowers. Building a brand requires clear, consistent messaging to your customer.

"When people in town think of lawn care, you want them to immediately think of your business," Phil said. "Right now, that's not happening. You haven't positioned yourself."

To get people to make that association, your brand has to be presented to them multiple times, and ideally in multiple ways. You have to use marketing and advertising to present your brand every way that you can — you have to hit them through mail, email, social media ads and internet advertisements. This can take years to do. Branding is the end-all be-all goal you are shooting for. Marketing or advertising is an avenue to get to the sale.

"One postcard maybe the tipping point for a customer that causes them to pick up the phone and buy from you, but at that point they are buying because you have brand awareness. Branding -- that's where you want to be, that's the long-term goal," Phil said. "That comes in the form of seeing your trucks with your logo on it, seeing the work you do, seeing you online, seeing you offline, hearing about you throughout the community and seeing your shop."

To create a brand, you need a logo and a website that represent your business and your industry, he said. It needs to be well designed and presented on your trucks and the team uniforms. It needs to capture what the company stands for as well — are you focused on affordability? Quality? Speed? Professionalism? The logo needs to be developed with a good design and colors that match the goal and mission of the business.

Also, to get a great brand, the central idea has to be able to stand on its own separate from the business owner, Phil told him. For Larry's Lawn Care, Larry is the brand. Whenever a customer has a problem, they are going to go asking for Larry. Everyone's always going to ask who Larry is, where he is and if they can talk with him.

"As you grow, gaining more jobs and more customers, it will be challenging to have your name in the company title because people will always feel they can complain to the owner, negotiate with the owner, and get special privileges if they talk to you directly," Phil explained. "That doesn't scale. Besides, if you ever want to sell your business it will be hard to explain that Larry is no longer the owner of "Larry's" Lawn Care."

"Okay, how do I start to build a brand? What do I start doing tomorrow?" Larry asked.

"Well, first off, you gotta change your business name," Phil said. "Then, you need to create a logo and a website. The reason you need to do that is for customers to see your brand in multiple areas. Finally, you need branded uniforms for your workers."

Right now, clients just see Larry's fliers, but they don't see any follow-up. There's no branding on his trucks, and no way to vet his company online by checking out customer reviews and pictures. Larry's business does not have the infrastructure necessary to build a brand, and to effectively market.

"Branding comes from having a plethora of punches in your arsenal and touching the customer multiple times, over and over again," Phil said.

"So once I have a logo and start building a brand, how do I actually create more business?" Larry asked.

"That's a great question," Phil said. "You need to advertise."

There are different types of media that you can pay for to reach a customer, he said. You can either rent advertising space or own it yourself. Renting media space is exemplified by paying for a print advertisement in a newspaper, or supporting a sports game in return for having your advertising presented there. You can rent social media space too. You place your picture, ad, or video on Facebook, Google, or other social media channels and pay for that space so that consumers see your products and services.

"Renting space gets immediate results because you're piggy-backing off of a large platform," Phil said. "But then, there is the option of owning your ad space—this way, you own the content. This is referred to as owned media."

Owned media comes is in the form of content you create. It can be videos, pictures, articles and testimonials that can be published on the company's website, online platforms, or in marketing campaigns.

"Basically, you create the content and distribute it to the customer," Phil said. "Instead of buying an ad in the local newspaper, you make the newspaper yourself and distribute it to customers and prospects. Instead of paying social media sites to share your pictures and videos, you create a blog on your website and disseminate your content via an email list you have created of all your customers and prospects."

With owned media, few eyeballs will see it until the business has grown and cultivated its brand. If you create a series of blog posts or videos on your website that show what you do, it is unlikely that you will have immediate traffic. However, you own those articles and content. Once they have been produced and published it takes very little money to maintain, and the content continues to bring in new customers. You don't have to keep paying over and over again to get your message out, as you do with newspaper ads, social media ads, and many other forms of "rented" attention.

Owned media is a long term strategy, and renting advertising space is a short-term strategy. With a few dollars, you can rent online advertising space that more people will see.

"In the short term, it really comes down to how much money you have. Marketing dollars add fuel to the fire for growing your business," Phil said. "If you have a ton of fuel, you can make the fire grow really fast, but the bottom line is that you are paying for it."

However, it's important to create owned media. Owning your content is part of a long-term branding strategy. But in the short-term sales side of things, businesses have to pay to rent advertising space to get their name out there.

"Facebook ads is currently a great social platform to be marketing on," Phil said. "You can generate leads, you can generate traffic to your website, you can generate phone calls and you can proliferate your pictures and videos of your jobs."

"Why is Facebook better than any other social media?" Larry asked.

"The beautiful thing about Facebook is that you can target people very specifically based upon their demographics, what they search for, what other pages they like, their age, their socioeconomic status and more," Phil said. "However, Facebook won't always be the best choice. In a few years, Facebook ads will get expensive and the ROI will be reduced. Rented space for advertising will constantly change with new forms of technology."

"So, what about advertising on Google or other search engines?" Larry asked.

"The awesome thing about advertising on web search, is that it is intent-based marketing," Phil explained. "People are looking for lawn care or landscaping and have actively started searching for your product or service. For this reason, your number of impressions will be lower and usually the cost per click is higher on Google or other search engines."

This strategy is different than with social media marketing. When advertising on social media, the business owner cannot determine whether the individual's being targeted are looking for their services. You are casting a big net and hoping some of the viewers have a need for your services. But with search engines, the people that see the advertisements are specifically looking for the product or service the business sells.

Renting space is a short-term thing, Phil explained. The platform will change and the cost of the leads will change. The long term play for marketing and advertising is owned media and content marketing.

Owned media content should be used to educate and to build a relationship between a business and its customers. For lawn care and landscaping businesses, educational owned media can be articles and videos about how to do something — how to mow a lawn, how and when to fertilize or how to install retaining walls. It can also take the form of newsletters and behind-the-scenes content showing the jobs you are doing and the team members you employ.

"The reason you educate the customer and tell them how to install their landscaping is not so much for the do-it-yourself person, it's more to show that you are the educator, and therefore the expert in your field," Phil said.

When a customer is reading a how-to article, they may follow the instructions and try to do something themselves, but more likely what will happen is that customer will realize that the business knows what they are doing. Then, when they need said services and they don't have time to do it themselves, the customer will call the business they learned from. You become the expert.

To build a relationship with a customer using owned media, businesses gather details about their customers and also share details about their business. This is called customer intelligence. Customer intelligence may include their email and their birthday, a milestone they are coming up to, a sickness in the family, or an upcoming vacation. These notes can be made in the CRM of your business and be used to communicate with Customers in an individualized and surprisingly personable way. Sharing information about your business with your customers can be done through email newsletters, handwritten thank you cards, and communication about your business goals and milestones. Make them part of the business... a fan that is rooting for your success.

"Owned media pays you in perpetuity," Phil said. "It's on your website forever, and it's always generating leads and awareness of your brand, as well as generating trust. Plus, you don't have to pay for it, because it's yours."

Branding is the long-term game. Owned media is the long-term game. You should be creating it from the beginning even if it doesn't get much attention, but it's going to get you where you want to in the long term.

Renting space is going to get you sales, it's going to get you leads, it's going to get in front of customers faster... but it is a treadmill of customer acquisition costs and should be used to grow the business until branding and content marketing catch up.

"Overall, your website is the greatest asset that you want to be working on — for branding purposes, and marketing purposes," Phil said. "However, print marketing is something you should also use."

Print marketing includes posters, fliers, and Every Door Direct Mail (EDDM). The EDDM strategy is through the United States Postal Service — instead of paying the cost a stamp, which is about 50 cents, you pay about 18 cents per delivered address. Mailers are sent to everyone in specific neighborhoods, and you get demographic data (such as age and income levels) about those neighborhoods that help you target more effectively. Print marketing is expensive, because each print piece has to be paid for, whether or not people are interested in the product or service. This is different than online social media and search engine marketing, where you only pay for the people clicking on it or viewing it — people who are interested. With print marketing you pay for the 95% of people who are going to throw it away without giving it a second look.

"You're basically using a big paint brush, and you're hoping something sticks," Phil said of print marketing. "Door hangers are great, some areas you can't do them though. Post cards are great, because they're cheap to print — fliers are great, too."

All of these options have pros and cons, and the most effective choice depends on your market. In one market, the newspaper might be the best place to advertise, while in another market you might not get a single lead. Every single market is different, but the bottom line is that you have to test different advertising channels and figure out what is best for your market.

"Figure out the Customer Acquisition Cost (CAC) of all the different mediums, and then double down on the one with the greatest Return On Investment (ROI)," Phil said. "Hopefully you remember us talking about this when we chatted about knowing your numbers."

"Wow… I have a lot to do," Larry said.

"You're leaving tonight," Phil said, leaning forward with earnestness. "Change your business name, create your logo and your website and work on those uniforms. Then, get back to me."

After Phil left, Larry laid back down in his bed and waited for the day to pass, with tons of thoughts and ideas swirling around in his mind. Big changes were coming.

CHAPTER 8: BACK AT SQUARE ONE

Larry, driving in his truck, pulled up to a local coffee shop and hopped out of the warm cabin into the chilly March air. It was starting to warm up outside, and the sun was higher in the sky, but the winter chill was still present. Larry gripped his coat and made his way inside. Phil was waiting for him at a booth next to the window. Smiling, he waved at him from his seat as Larry approached. Phil shook his hand.

"Larry, you're looking well!" he said, like they were best friends reuniting.

"I'm feeling well," Larry said. "I have so much to tell you."

"I hope so, what have you done in the last six months?" Phil asked.

Larry went into detail about all he has accomplished since he last saw Phil at the hospital, his chest welling up with pride as he spoke. Throughout that time, Larry had taken all of Phil's advice word for word.

He first picked up the phone and called Pedro to ask him if he wanted to continue working with him. Larry hadn't talked to him since the accident, because things were so hectic. He remembered crossing his fingers hoping Pedro wanted to stick with him, and Larry explained how that phone call went to Phil.

"So, basically I called up Pedro. I asked how he was doing. He was healed up by then," Larry said. "I told him I had a new vision for the business, and that I wanted him to become more than just a laborer — I wanted him to be my operations manager."

"What did he think of that?" Phil asked.

"He was really excited. He was stoked that the company had plans to grow, and that it wouldn't just be me and him driving around anymore," Larry said, chuckling to himself a bit.

Larry changed the name of his business, too. Long gone was Larry's Lawn Care — his new business name was **Augusta Lawn Care Services**. Once Larry changed the name of his business, he looked at how to present it. He remembered that Phil told him he needed a well-designed logo, and that it needed to be presented on everything from his fliers to his trucks and uniforms.

He wanted to make sure the logo was attractive, and that it was representative of his business, so he researched everything he could about it. He ended up designing a logo using the colors yellow, green and brown. Each color was chosen for specific reasons. The brown is a color that evokes trust. The green represents the earth and ecology. The yellow represents vitality.

With his new name and logo, Larry worked on building a website for his company. Without much technology experience, he was nervous about the prospect of creating a website. He discovered that it wasn't as daunting as he had thought — there were a number of services available that helped him build a website without having any web development knowledge. He picked a website builder, purchased a domain and hooked it all up, bringing augustalawncareservices.com live within the first week being home from the hospital.

The website included an "About Us" page, which described the business and it's journey, explaining how long they've been in business and his credentials. He also added a page for contacting the business. Throughout the following months, Larry collected customer reviews, pictures and videos that he published online.

"The owned media stuff has already been super helpful," he told Phil. "People are telling me that they watched my videos, or checked out our customer reviews before choosing to go with Augusta."

With insurance money he received after the car accident, Larry bought another truck, but he chose an inexpensive yet reliable used one. He got rid of his open-air trailer, and replaced it with an enclosed one. Larry branded his trucks and his trailer with vinyl graphics, including his business logo, website and phone number.

Because his business was more visible than ever, Larry started generating new leads quickly. With all the new customers, he needed to work on an improved estimating process that was more efficient. He started by writing a pricing matrix for his estimates, which gave him a dollar-per-man-hour charge. When Larry would do his estimates, he determined how many hours the job would take, plus the cost of materials, and charged the customer based on those costs. No longer was it a guessing game. He ended up putting his rate-per-man-hour at $60 — a dollar per minute. This was almost 50% more than he was charging before.

He also created a menu of standardized prices for installing different materials and for equipment rentals. For example, he had prices per square foot on sod, price per pound of fertilizer and price per square foot for mowing. Since these prices were standardized, he made them available to his customers on his website as well. The prices were listed at www.augustalawncareservices.com/our-pricing.

For mowing, Larry had come up with a very efficient estimating process. He realized that with his square foot standard prices, all he had to do was find out the area of a property, and he could name a price. Larry started using satellite maps to drop pins on properties and find out how many square feet the area of lawn was — that way, he didn't even have to visit the site. That saved him from driving all over the place to price mowing jobs, and allowed the crew to be the ones using the trucks.

With his transparent pricing matrix available to customers online, he noticed that fewer customers tried to haggle with him. Larry now knows how much it costs him to do a job, and he knows exactly what his profit margins are.

"It's crazy, customers don't try low-balling me anymore," Larry said, taking a sip of his coffee.

"That's one of the benefits of having standardized prices," Phil said. "It's like when you go to McDonalds.

You never haggle about the price of the cheeseburger because you know the person before and after you are all paying the same price that is made publicly visible on the menu."

With Pedro as his right-hand man, Larry went out and hired more workers, constantly growing his team. He hired four to five more guys. He did this by creating his very own career fair nights. He would advertise the career fair online and make the applicants fill out an online form. Only eligible applicants that passed certain requirements were invited to attend. He screened out people who weren't legally able to work in the United States, and people with criminal or drug histories using the questionnaire.

Only about half of the invited applicants even showed up to the career fair, which helped further weed out low-performing employees. During the career fair presentations, Larry explained the history of the company and his goals for the future of the company. He described the pros and cons of working out in the field, the working environment and the business culture. He described his expectations for new employees, and told them what they could expect from him as the owner.

Larry's goal was to scare off individuals that couldn't work hard, couldn't keep up the pace and wouldn't be adaptable to the culture he was trying to create. He set up interviews with people of interest, and people who remained interested in working for him, after meeting them at the career fairs. During interviews, he made sure to get references, and he would ask specifically what previous employers would say about the applicant's performance.

"I never ask them what their previous employers *would* say *if* I call, I always ask them what *will* they say *when* I call," Larry explained. "I've found that it makes them answer more honestly, because they know I will actually speak with their previous employer."

"That's great, it sounds like you have found great guys," Phil said. "What was your first new hire like?"

Larry described his first addition to the crew. The first great laborer he found to work with Pedro out in the field actually had no experience with lawn care. However, he had been working for a fast food restaurant consistently for about five years, and had great references. He was teachable, and good with customer service, so Larry hired him. The experience at the franchise made him adapt well to the systems-dependent environment Larry sought to achieve.

"Oh, I forgot to mention, my whole crew has branded uniforms too," Larry said with a wink. "They almost look better than yours."

Phil laughed.

"So, what do you think?" Larry asked.

"It sounds like you're off to a really good start. You're experiencing some incredible growth," he said. "I think it's time for you to get an office manager. It's time to get someone to start taking things off your plate — you've done a great job getting out of the field, but now you need to focus on the things that are going to scale up the business."

Augusta Lawn Care Services had revenues of between $30,000 to $40,000 a month at this point, depending on the time of year. Larry was gearing up for spring.

"The next step is really to get someone to answer emails and phone calls. It's going to hurt your profit margins in the short term, since their time is not billable hours and they are an overhead expenses, but it will really pay off in the long term," Phil explained.

Phil stressed the importance of creating systems for the office manager to follow so that they didn't have to ask Larry what to do all of the time. If the office manager is supposed to intercept phone calls and emails and respond to them for Larry, it wouldn't be useful for him if the manager called him each time a customer had a question and asked what to say or how to respond.

"Also, when you get towards the winter with all of your new employees, you need a strategy to keep them busy," Phil warned. "Think about services you can offer. And remember, it's not really about making money during the winter, it's about keeping your crew busy so they don't go on unemployment or leave for another job. You don't want to have to cycle through new crew members every year. It's bad for culture and hard to build a solid team if that happens every year."

"Gosh, that's a good point... what sort of Winter services can I offer besides the stuff I already do?" Larry asked, intrigued.

"I know landscapers who focus on pressure washing, snow plowing and salting, gutter cleaning, tree services and such," Phil said. "I've even heard of companies offering janitorial services in the winter, and handyman services too."

"Okay, I'll put some thought into that," Larry said. "Phil, I can't thank you enough for all of your help. You've really helped turn my business around."

"Larry, you did that yourself. I just helped you learn how," Phil said, standing up to leave. He threw a cash tip on the table, and they walked out of the coffee shop together.

Phil looked out at Larry's not-so-new truck in the parking lot.

"It looks great man," he said.

Larry was happy to hear it. They shook hands and parted ways, promising to keep in touch.

CHAPTER 9: A NEW BUSINESS, A NEW MINDSET

It was Monday morning. Larry woke up to see leaves falling from the trees outside of his apartment — it was November. Savannah was sleeping, but their new baby had woken up, so Larry got up to tend to him. They named him Charles, and he was now a healthy four-month-old. Before leaving for work that morning, he kissed Savannah on the forehead, which woke her up.

"Have a good day at work," she said, yawning.

Larry ran down the stairs and hopped into his truck, turning the key until the engine fired up and backed out of his driveway to head to his new business office. He pulled up to his rented storage facility, which was located in an industrial area, and had his Augusta Lawn Care trucks parked there. With the extra crew and space, Larry had a lot more equipment. The facility also included a small office room, where his new office manager Andrea was waiting for him when he walked in.

"Good morning Larry," she said. "I didn't get a chance to chat with you last Friday about a customer issue, let me catch you up on what happened before the meeting."

"Oh yeah? What's the deal?" he asked.

"The Brady's had their trees trimmed while they were out of town, but when they got home and saw, the work they are not super happy with it," Andrea said.

"They called and said the trees looked a bit ragged, and that we didn't trim enough off. Also, the crew left some debris on the ground."

"Was it fixed last week?" Larry said.

"Oh yeah. It was actually Pedro's mistake. He went out and fixed it that night, and you'll hear all about it at the meeting," Andrea said.

As the company grew over the past year and Larry had hired on new workers, he saw that he needed a system to promote accountability. With seven workers now on the crew Larry wanted them to take pride in their work and prevent silly mistakes. He created a system for accountability and customer service complaints. Prior to his system being implemented Larry didn't really have a way to target one worker for making a mistake, while helping them improve. He created the yellow slip system to help address this.

The way it worked was that when there was a customer issue, Andrea would track down which crew member had performed the service at the customer's property. She would write their name on the slip, as well as the client's name and the complaint. That person, within 48 hours, has to return to the client's property and talk to them in-person while resolving the issue. Once they did that, the crew member would write down how they resolved the issue on the slip and then present it to the rest of the crew at the next Monday team meeting.

Monday morning meetings were called scoreboard huddles. The company's scoreboard was another new system Larry implemented. It was a visual representation of whether the team is "winning" or "losing." The scoreboard tracks monthly revenue, monthly efficiency, sales, yellow slips and damage cases. They also had team meetings on Wednesdays, where team building exercises, motivation, personal development, and leadership cultivation were the topics of discussion. Larry would show a video or read something from a book, then the team would discuss how that certain topic related to Augusta Lawn Care and improving the business.

Collected monthly revenue is shown on the scoreboard, and compared to the monthly revenue goal. Monthly efficiency is tracked through a dollar per man hour metric — Larry would take the weekly revenue and divide it by the total hours on payroll, including estimator and office manager hours, which gave him a dollar per hour rate. To easily see how efficient the team was working, Larry made the scoreboard with a graphic of a traffic light... red, yellow and green. If the team was hitting $50 or more per hour, then they were in the green zone on the board. Between $40 and $50 per hour was considered the yellow zone, and under $40 was the red zone. The board also tracked equipment damage cases and yellow slips, and gave the team a good indicator of how well the business was running that week, and through the month.

A scoreboard in a sports event is a visual reminder of where you are at in the game, which is exactly what was shown on the company scoreboard. The scoreboard you make for your team should be quick and easy to read and allow team members to quickly see if they are winning or losing… and how far along in the game they are.

The scoreboard tracked sales and included how many new mowing customers and landscaping jobs they got each week. Damage cases included the number of incidents in which something was broken, whether it was the company's equipment, or part of a clients property.

The crew was starting to file into the storage facility to begin the Monday morning Scoreboard Huddle. During the meeting, Pedro presented his yellow slip, and explained what he did to fix it. Right after Andrea told him about the complaint Friday evening, Pedro took the extra time to go fix the trees. He didn't get home until 8 p.m. that night, but the customers were happy. After Pedro was done with his presentation, Larry reminded the crew that this could happen to any of them since the client was not present at the end of the job to inspect the work.

"Alright, so remember to do walk-throughs after finishing up your job," Larry told the group. "If you get a yellow slip, you're going to be the one going back and fixing it, and going home late is never fun. Besides, it's a whole lot easier to satisfy a client at the end of the job, than when you have a yellow slip, they have complained, and you are embarrassed."

After Pedro's presentation, they looked over the scoreboard. The business was struggling a bit with efficiency this month, and they were in the yellow. Larry posed the issue to the crew, and asked them to come up with ideas for improving efficiency.

"We could hook up the equipment in the evenings instead of in the morning," one team member said. "Most of the time in the morning we are all slow, because we just woke up. In the evenings, we want to get home as fast as possible, so I bet we would get the equipment ready way faster."

"That's a great idea," another said. "I think that would be better for everyone."

Larry smiled, realizing he had employees that cared about the business, and were engaged in this process.

"Sounds good to me. We will see if it improves our efficiency. Any more ideas how we could get into the green this coming week?" Larry asked.

More ideas started flowing into the conversation after that. The next best idea was to incorporate an equipment checklist system so that everyone had exactly what they needed each day, and didn't need to return to the shop between jobs to pick up stuff they needed. *"These guys know exactly where they can save time,"* Larry thought, impressed by their ingenuity and knowing that they were the ones that were in the trenches every day seeing the inefficiencies.

He remembered back when he used to work for Joe, and how different the culture was. Everyone who worked there was usually unsatisfied with something, and they weren't super engaged in the performance of the business. They just showed up and did their job, and so did Larry. *"I've really got a good team here,"* he thought to himself. Most of them had never worked in lawn care and landscaping, but they were all team players. On top of that, they were honest, trustworthy people.

After the meeting was over and everyone left to start their routes, Larry went back to the office with Andrea. There was a part of his business that he hadn't tackled for a while, and he needed come up with a way to improve it.

"Okay, we need to create a better system for how estimates are created, and really focus on converting leads into customers," Larry said. "We need to improve our closing ratio, basically."

Larry's current system used a Customer Relationship Management (CRM) system through a mobile app, which allowed him to get his schedule on his phone. When he goes to a job, he would write the notes for that estimate in the app. On landscaping estimates he itemized the cost of each aspect of the job, but on mowing jobs Andrea was able to do estimates from the office by calculating the square footage of a property, and using that to build a price. So basically, Larry had to physically show up at properties when customers wanted landscaping done.

With that extra effort, Larry wanted to improve the likelihood that those landscaping estimates produce a customer. To do that, he needed to continually remind that customer, from the first point of contact to asking for a review after the job was completed, that his company offered professional, quality service.

"I'm thinking we should spend some money on nice, cardstock introduction packets that I can hand out to those potential landscaping clients," Larry said. "That way we are spending money on people that are already close to buying, instead of using that money to reel in more cold leads through marketing and advertising."

"That makes sense. It's just like you said, let's improve our closing ratio," Andrea said. "I think that's a good idea."

The packet would have a bunch of information about the company: how they got started, what services they provide, recent customer reviews with pictures of completed jobs and so forth. The pages would also sit in a nice cardstock packet, making it look as professional as possible.

"We'll be spending money on people who have already called, already made contact and presented themselves as a potential customers… you know, warm leads," Larry reaffirmed. "That way we're not always focusing on cold leads and new business."

He also wanted to streamline his landscape estimate process. He planned to have Andrea complete the cost estimates with materials and man hours from the office, so he didn't have to do that out in the field. She could use his job notes from the app and the company's pricing structure to determine costs based on materials and labor hours.

"I'd like to see estimates scheduled within 24 hours of the phone call, and sent to the customer within 24 hours of the the appointment," Larry said. "If you start doing a lot of those calculations and setting up the landscaping estimate from the office, rather than me doing calculations on the property, then we can get estimates out faster."

"Wow, and I thought we were already fast," Andrea said. "Most companies take like a week. But if we start implementing this process I think we can easily do it."

"I've got another big idea, too," Larry said. "This will be for every estimate."

He explained his new plan to improve the customers experience, and hopefully lure more people into accepting estimates. Once Andrea is done calculating and writing up an estimate, Larry thought she should use her phone to create a personalized, 30-second video explaining that she is sending over the estimate and that the she can get them on the schedule right away. In the video Andrea would mention the customer's name, a description of the job and tell the customer to call with any questions. She would quickly shoot the video on her phone, upload it to YouTube (unlisted) and embed it in the email sent to the customer. The email would show up with a link to the estimate, as well as a link to her video. This personalized touch will make the customer know that the video was made just for them… not just a generic video created for all prospects.

"So at that point, the customer would get a packet, a personalized video from the office explaining that the estimate is handed off to you, Andrea, and you can tell them that when they accept, a project manager will take over the job from there," he said. "That shows we've invested time and effort into providing them quick, quality service, and lets them know how the process works and which team member will be taking care of them. By the time the job is started they have seen the estimator, the office manager, and the project manager and have been guided through the process of when each person is handling their job."

Clicking on the estimate link brings the customer to an online client portal that shows them all of their payment information, invoices, past and present. It also allows them to have their credit card on file. The estimate link includes a button that says "Accept," which automatically notifies the office that the job needs to get scheduled and has the proposal has been accepted.

After the job proposal has been accepted, Andrea would send another video thanking the customer, and if the job was over $3,000, she would explain that they need to provide a 50% deposit. If it was a recurring job such as mowing, she would go over the scheduled work dates, and so on.

With the CRM, automatic emails are sent to customers automatically based on certain actions. Once the customer accepts an estimate, the CRM would automatically send a "Welcome to the Family" email and an email that asks the customer to put their credit card on file.

"So as we go forward, we want to also focus on upselling the customers we've done business with in the past," Larry concluded. "That way we get the most out of the customers that we have and increase the lifetime value of the customer"

Andrea had been creating a monthly email newsletter for a few months, so Larry focused in on that.

"Your newsletters are a great tool to keep customers engaged," Larry said. "Let's make sure to promote our work in every email. Like right now, its fall, so you could market our fall cleanup services in the newsletter."

"So like fall cleanups, leaf clean-ups and tree trimming services?" Andrea said.

"Yes, definitely." Larry said.

Andrea started putting together the email newsletter that day, and she included pricing details of each fall-specific job. She made it visually engaging, with colors and imagery, and included videos of their recent work. She sent it over to Larry before the end of the day, and he checked it before heading home.

Larry responded to her email, telling her she did a great job. She emailed back with a link to a video, which showed Andrea closing up the office.

"Glad you like it Larry, have a good night!" she said.

"Wow, she's already got it down," Larry thought.

CHAPTER 10: GOING BEYOND LAWN CARE SERVICES

Larry was sitting in the office looking over his finances while Andrea was busy at work. As he skimmed over the numbers, he thought to himself, *"How can I make sure we aren't strapped for cash next spring?"* It was January of his third year of business under the name Augusta Lawn Care, and they had managed to get through most of the winter without any debt, but this spring the business wouldn't have any money to invest. He'd burnt through it. Larry wanted to come up with a plan that could help propel the business through the cold months without fear of finances, but also allow him to better prepare for spring.

The last few winters usually caused Larry to lose a lot of cash, and when spring would roll around, he never had enough capital to make investments for the summer. He wanted to buy more trucks, hire more people and grow his business, but every time spring and summer would come, the business lacked funds to do so.

In his mind, Larry heard Phil's words.

"When you get towards the winter with all of your new employees, you need a strategy to keep them busy."

A strategy. He needed a strategy.

Larry tapped his fingers against his desk, running through the examples Phil had given him. There was pressure washing, snow plowing and salting, gutter cleaning, tree services, handyman services, so many different options....

But then, Larry realized he didn't have to pick one service. He could offer multiple. His crew was talented, and they all were fast learners. Labor was their strong suit. If Larry could put their labor to use in the winter, for things other than lawn care, he could come into spring next year with cash to spare. In an ah-ha moment, Larry stood up abruptly.

"Andrea!" he said. "I have a plan for next winter. We are going to get the guys working doing handyman stuff, helping people move, home repairs, assembling furniture and electronics, junk removal... you name it."

"Sounds cool," she said, surprised by the sudden outburst.

"We're gonna call it... Pro Labor Services," Larry said with a smile.

Letting his excitement fuel him, Larry took to the computer to start creating his new winter business. He designed a logo and created a website, www.prolaborservices.com, and by the end of January, he had a fully-fledged winter strategy that would keep the crew busy, as well as preserve his cash for the following spring. Larry emailed clients that week and started advertising the service, and was able to book out his crew for the rest of the winter.

Now that he had launched Pro Labor Services, he hoped it could sustain his entire crew through the next winter and keep his cash flow balanced. Larry knew his per hour rate was not as profitable as his lawn care rates of about $60 per hour, but it would be enough to keep everyone paid and keep cash flow at least breaking even throughout the Winter.

This time of the year, many other lawn care and landscaping companies are laying people off. Larry knew that. With the ability to keep his crew busy for the rest of the winter doing various handyman and labor work, Larry realized he could afford to pick up a few more crew members. *"Hiring right now is perfect,"* he thought. *"I can find guys that already know what they're doing and are being laid off due to the seasonality of lawn care."* Larry was able to hire a few more people, swiping them away from his competitors, when February rolled around.

Larry's horizons had opened for next year, because he realized he would now have the ability to make big moves before spring — a crucial point in time that can help set up a lawn care business for success for the rest of the year. He could plan to buy more trucks and hire even more people. No longer would Augusta Lawn Care be constrained by cash because of long, unproductive Winters.

With this in mind, Larry began dreaming about growth. He wanted to get to over a million per year in revenue. *"Okay, if I want to grow, I need a plan,"* Larry thought. That meant he needed to create a budget, and he needed to plan for about 40% growth.

Sitting down in his office, Larry started brainstorming. There were questions to answer: How many people would Larry need working for him? How many mowing customers would he need? How much more equipment would he need? How much space would he need? Larry started running the numbers, and determined he would need 100 more mowing customers to reach his goal, and he would need to hire five more people, plus an office person. He also needed to get three more trucks, another trailer and mowing set-up. More office space and parking would also be necessary.

Looking forward at the year ahead, Larry planned out how he was going to hire new crew members and purchase equipment. He was going to hire two people in March, one person in May, and another person in June. For his trucks, Larry figured he could get one truck in March, one truck in April and one truck in May — then he'd be set for the rest of the year. He would purchase the additional trailer and mowing set-up mid-summer, and by August, he would have the cash needed for more shop space, according to Larry's growth plan.

All of these needs cost money. Larry needed to budget out how much cash each action required, and then make sure he allocated his funds correctly so that he had what he needed to hire two people in March and buy a truck, for example. This required building up those additional 100 customers, and making more sales. Larry needed a marketing plan, along with a budget, to help get him those additional customers.

Larry started by breaking down the year into months so he could determine what his marketing focus would be at different points in time. March was coming up, and he knew that during March, April and May, they would really be hitting hard on mowing services. Into May, there would be an increased focus on fertilization and weed control, then throughout the summer they would then switch more to upselling add-on services to existing customers — clean-ups, bush trimming, weed control, fertilization packages — then through the dry months, July and August, irrigation services and artificial turf would be the focus. That time of the year would also be the time to push xeriscaping, which is a form of reducing the water needs for lawn maintenance.

Into the fall, September and October, he knew there would be a focus on fall clean-ups and moss control as the weather dampens. He would start pitching sprinkler blowouts to customers, and later into October and November, leaf clean-ups would be the big thing. Into December and January, Larry would focus on tree trimming. This time of the year, when deciduous trees have lost their leaves, is the best time to prune them. In January and February, he planned to push Pro Labor Services to his clients… a time when landscape jobs are usually sparse.

During these winter months, Larry would offer services discounted. That would be the ONLY time he would offer discounted services. The stuff he would advertise as discounted would be hardscaping projects, such as retaining walls, which can be done in the winter.

With all these services laid out by month, Larry began coming up with a marketing plan. In the spring (March-April-May), he came up with a door hanger marketing strategy. The idea was to hang advertising door hangers on the doors of houses closest to his other customers, to hopefully facilitate denser, more efficient mowing routes. If he could get as many people to become customers in one neighborhood as possible, his crew could save time and money because it would cut down travel time between jobs. He also would focus on targeted marketing through Every Door Direct Mail (EDDM), further emphasizing the importance of route density and efficiency. Larry cast a wider net online using Facebook ads and Google Adwords to attract new customers from throughout his entire local community.

Spring would be the time to allocate most of his marketing dollars. It's the best time of the year to focus on customer acquisition. With this in mind, Larry decided to spend about 60% or more of his marketing dollars during spring. The other nine months out of the year would be mostly focused on upselling existing customers, rather than acquiring new ones.

Larry leaned back in his chair and took in all of his work. It was a laundry list of numbers and dollar signs, neatly organized in a spreadsheet. It took into account all of his income and expenses, and gave Larry a roadmap for how he would spend capital this year. He took a deep breath and relaxed, knowing that he wouldn't be going into the next year of business blind. He had a plan... a strategy.

CHAPTER 11: THE FINISH LINE

Larry walked into his new house one evening to five-year-old James running up and greeting him at the entryway. James slammed into Larry's shins and wrapped his arms around his dad's legs.

"Daddy!" he giggled.

Larry picked him up and held him on his hip walking into the living room, where Savannah and Charles, who was over a year and a half old, were coloring with crayons. Savannah looked up and smiled. She got Charles' attention.

"Hey buddy, look, dad's home," she said in a soft voice.

Larry plopped James back on the floor, who ran off, and sat down with Charles and Savannah, giving them each a kiss. They talked about their day, and discussed dinner plans. As Larry was talking, he started to think about how different their lives were five years ago.

Back then, Larry had just started his new business, and it was named after himself. He was struggling to make ends meet, living in a small apartment with a new baby. He ran through the first year of Larry's Lawn Care in his mind — that week without work his first winter, hiring his first employee Brad, then Melvin, then firing them both. He thought about how hard he worked after that trying to do the work of three guys all by himself. He remembered his sickness, losing weight, and getting to the point where Savannah was scared for him.

Then there was Pedro. Hiring Pedro saved his business and his body during the following year. They were a great team, and things started to look up, but the business was still on very shaky ground. Getting into the car accident changed everything. *"I don't know where I would be right now if I had never met Phil,"* Larry thought. Phil kept his business afloat while Pedro and Larry recovered, and Phil taught Larry how to build a successful business.

Now, Larry had a business that could stand on its own. It was no longer Larry's Lawn Care — it was Augusta Lawn Care Services. He also had a winter business, Pro Labor Services, that kept his whole crew busy when business got slow. Larry's business had a logo and a website, and all of his equipment was branded with contact information. He was marketing and advertising to clients in an effective way, which meant he was always gaining new clients, and always growing using his content marketing strategy.

He was still working a lot, and there were still problems to be solved every single day. Things would break, employees would leave, customers would complain. Larry was constantly fighting fires, day in and day out. However, there was a lot less stress, and his business was more stable. His business was systems-centric, no longer personality centric.

Larry now knows what to expect in terms of revenue, customers and employees. When he comes home in the evenings, there's no longer the fear of where the next job is coming from, and wondering if he will be able to do the work. There's people in place, and plans that work. Larry always knows what to expect, and he has created a team that has leaders within it. His employees don't need to come to him anymore for their questions, which means he's no longer the bottleneck for everything in terms of scheduling, hiring and daily operations. Larry has created systems that run themselves, and hired great people keep things moving.

It is now possible for Larry to truly take a vacation, because he knows his business will continue to run. However, the family hasn't taken advantage of this newfound freedom. Larry remembered back to the last vacation the family took, before Charles was born, and how Melvin and Brad were incapable of keeping the business going. He realized now he had set them up for failure.

Larry hasn't solved all the problems in his industry, though. In the past few years, Larry was lucky to find good people that make his success possible. But he hasn't kept all of them, even though he wanted to. He's lost employees, and had to rehire people, which means he has continually had to get new hires trained up. *"It's still hard to keep a team, keep them motivated,"* he thought to himself, realizing that would probably never change. *"There's always going to be people who think they aren't being paid enough, or think they are being treated unfairly."* But Larry has a couple of project managers and a lawn care manager, an office manager and some assistants, and they have been loyal to the business. They have provided structure, and helped soften the blow of laborer turnover.

That night, laying in bed, Larry turned to Savannah before falling asleep.

"I can't believe how far we've come," he whispered.

She sighed, looking back at him. "I know."

They fell asleep that night grateful for everything they had achieved together. Savannah and Larry woke up on Saturday morning, getting ready for a day with the kids. They had homemade pancakes and scrambled eggs for breakfast, and hung out at the house. After breakfast, Larry took a cup of coffee over to his computer, and decided to start going through customer reviews. He'd been curious about what people were saying, but hadn't had a chance to look through customer feedback.

After going through at least 100 comments and reviews online, and he noticed a pattern. Almost everything he read, whether it was good or bad, had to do with the customer's experience, rather than the actual work. Very few of them talked about the work they did, as much as how the work was done and the experience of working with Augusta Lawn Care and the team of staff. *"People are not buying what we do,"* he realized. *"They're buying how and why we do it."*

This was good news to Larry. In the past couple of years, he had become obsessed with customer experience. Customer experience was part of the reason he had Andrea send videos to prospects, create an email newsletter for customers, and automate follow-up systems for jobs. But that was just the beginning.

He started diving into every single detail of experience, from the begin stage of the relationship (seeing their trucks, seeing the crew in uniform, seeing them on jobsites) to the end of the job (doing a walkthrough, taking payment). Larry also focused on his company's message, and how Augusta Lawn Care was talked about in the community. He was continually tweaking the website to perfect the online experience, too. Search Engine Optimization (SEO) and content creation was a constant work in progress but the colors, design, and flow of the site was given special care and thought.

Larry didn't think about the element of customer interaction within his business as "customer service." He saw customer service as an overused term, and one that looks backward rather than forward. Customer service is usually used to solve a problem of the past. Larry thinks about the customer element in his business in terms of "customer experience" instead — this idea looks forward to the future. What will customers see, feel and smell when interacting with the company? What is the vibe they will experience? Do they see the company as a large fortune 500 corporation, or as a small mom and pop shop? How the customer perceives the business plays a large role in customer satisfaction. If customer experience is focused on, customer service takes care of itself.

Some customer experience changes he made that were effective were also small. For instance, Larry had been charging a fee for customers to pay using a credit card. They had to pay 3% to cover the processing fees. But then, one of his customers pointed out that Larry was penalizing the customers that spend the most. He was basically tacking on an additional 3% fee for customers spending $1,000 or more with Augusta Lawn Care. After that customer pointed out the issue, Larry realized he was penalizing his biggest customers, and that was detrimental to business — so he removed the fee, and he made it possible for customers to put their credit cards on file with the business, and autopay for monthly charges or large one-time installs.

One change he was proud of involved the connection his business formed with customers. Larry wanted to finds meaningful ways to thank his clients for choosing Augusta Lawn Care, so he came up with an idea for a new customer experience system. He began sending out signed thank you cards to customers with completed jobs, and the cards showed a picture of the team, along with handwritten signatures. He constantly thought about ways he could surprise and delight the customer at each interaction.

Larry made sure that customers always knew exactly what to expect too, as well as what step they were in the process of a job. His estimating system gave clients a heads-up on the entire process at each step of the way — after the first phone call, Andrea would book an estimate time with the new client, explaining that an estimator will show up and look over the jobsite. Then, once that step was done, they let the customer know they could expect to see their estimate emailed to them within 24 hours. After that, they would get an email with all the information on what happens once they accept, neatly and concisely explained in a customized video by Andrea. It all worked like clockwork.

At this point in his business development, Larry had assumed the role of the C.E.O. His job became polishing the systems that were put in place. He constantly reviewed systems and checked for problems he could solve. He also was more and more involved in training and motivating his team during Monday and Wednesday meetings. Larry followed the concept of open-book management, which means he kept every employee in the loop on how the business used finances. This strategy allowed the employees to buy into the purpose and goals of the business. The transparency helped the culture of the company to be one of trust and common purpose.

As Larry continued to read through customer reviews that Saturday morning, he realized that a lot of his work growing a company culture and creating systems for customer experience had paid off. This was the stuff that customers and employees care about.

Larry finished his coffee and shut off the computer, but his mind was still focused on his business. The family went to the park that day and had a picnic together. Later that night, Larry decided to go see his new office space. He went by himself.

Driving in his truck, he pulled up to the building he now owned. Turning off the engine, he stayed in his seat for a while, looking out the window at the shop. After a few minutes, he got up and opened the door, causing the truck to alert until the door was closed again.

He slowly walked up the few steps to the front door, opening it up. No one was working this Saturday afternoon. The office was clean and spacious, and he could see his equipment neatly put away from the window. There was plenty of parking space, and the whole facility seemed well-maintained.

The evening sun was streaming into the office as he stood there admiring the fruits of his labor. It almost glowed. Larry realized his whole outlook on life had changed — his viewpoint towards family, towards time, towards people and towards his business. He had become more of a giving person; a mentor for his team. He had become the father he had always wanted, spending time with his kids more than ever before. He had become successful… for success is achieved by the person who has attained contentment. Larry's Lawn Care was a thing of the past. Larry's old life was a thing of the past.

ABOUT THE AUTHOR

Mike Andes has been in the landscaping industry for 12 years. He teaches landscapers how to grow their business and achieve $100,000 a month in revenue through his online course and podcast (LandscapeBusinessCourse.com).

Mike is the founder of Augusta Lawn Care Services (AugustaLawnCareServices.com) and Pro Labor Services (ProLaborServices.com). He also owns an Anytime Fitness gym and hosts the podcast " Business Bootcamp Podcast," where he helps entrepreneurs from all industries start, grow, and save their businesses.

For more information and insight concerning lawn care and landscaping business advice check out Landscape Business Course on your podcast player, online, or on YouTube & Facebook. You can join our private Facebook group or even attend our live conference to meet Mike in-person!

Made in United States
Orlando, FL
18 August 2022

21165469R00078